Linked Lives

A MEMOIR OF AN EXTRAORDINARY 40-YEAR FRIENDSHIP

Bonny Brookes

Bonny Brookes

DEDICATION

Dedicated in memory of my dear friend,
Lori Jane

To the man who loved her unconditionally,
Steve

And, to my wonderful godchildren,
Lisa and Jason

CONTENTS

ACKNOWLEDGMENTS

There are many people to thank, but to these special ones, I am deeply grateful: Mikaela, Nancy, Grace, Chris, Steve, Lisa, Jason, Danielle, Mike, Sandra, Alex, Jim, Weymon, Rhys, Linda, Katharine, Dolores, and especially, Lori.
Without you, your help, support and love this book might never have been. Thank you all.

Bonny Brookes

PRELUDE

A single tear rolled slowly down my cheek. With the back of my hand, I wiped it off, took a deep breath and began speaking.

I looked around the room at a sea of mourners. Some sat quietly, others openly wept. All these lives linked to Lori. She had loved them all.

Some people come into our lives for a moment, while others remain with us for a lifetime. Lori and I shared a lifetime. She was not rich, nor was she famous, but her life made a difference to those she loved . . . including me. This is our story.

1
INNOCENCE

The day after my graduation from eighth grade in 1972, I sprang out of bed eager to start summer vacation. After the daily household chores were completed, I could do whatever I wanted—well, within reason, of course. I decided to jump on my bike and go visit school friends that lived in the neighborhood.

Only seven years earlier, the neighborhood had been a farmer's field. Today, two-story brick houses, with a few tri-levels mixed in, stood in the place of cornstalks. Most of the young maple and elm trees, planted at the time the homes were built, stood about ten feet high bursting with early summer foliage. Many homes sported front flower gardens adding splashes of pink, red, orange and yellow to the bright green manicured lawns.

I spotted some girls sitting in a circle on the front lawn a few houses down and pulled my bike up next to them. I had known all but one of these girls since fourth grade. The unfamiliar girl had hair the color of wheat that fell to the middle of her back and she wore big round glasses over her hazel eyes. Her slim physique reminded me of the cartoon character, Olive Oyl. I smiled at her, then joined in the conversation about school, the boys, the girls, and later on, about everyone's plans on what they wanted to do over the summer. I also learned this girl, Lori, wasn't new to the neighborhood. She attended parochial school and since I attended public school, that's why we'd never met before.

Soon mothers called for their daughters to come home for lunch.

When only Lori and I remained seated cross-legged on the grass, I asked her, "Do you have to go home too?"

"No."

"Does your mom work? My mom works at RCA."

"Both my parents work down at our drugstore."

"Your parents own a drugstore?"

Lori looked embarrassed. "Yeah."

"That's cool! My dad owns a company too, but his work is boring and he's gone all the time. He's an insurance adjuster. I think being at a drugstore all day would be a lot more fun."

I looked down the street toward the house I lived in with my mother, father and brother. We'd moved here from Iowa five years before, to be closer to my mother's family.

I wondered if I'd get into trouble for inviting Lori over without Mother being there. My little brother would probably rat me out, but I decided to invite her anyway. "Hey, would you like to come over to my house?" I asked pointing it out. "I could make us some sandwiches."

"Sure, Bon," Lori said. I pushed my bike along as Lori and I walked. Once inside, we climbed the stairs and peeked into my brother's room. Scott was completely opposite of me with his blue/green eyes, blond hair and introverted personality. He sat on the floor creating something with his *Erector Set* and didn't notice us go by.

Lori and I entered my room and found my cat, Thomasina, on the bed, calmly bathing herself. "That's Tommy," I pointed to my cat with one hand as I picked up the phone with the other. "Just sit on my bed. I need to call my mom to make sure it's okay that you're here."

Lori held out her hand for the cat to sniff, "Hi Tommy." She petted Thomasina and looked around the room until I hung up the phone.

"My mom said you can stay, but said you needed to call your mom and let her know where you are."

"Okay." As Lori spoke with her mother, I closed my bedroom door revealing posters of Davy Jones, Bobby Sherman and David Cassidy.

"She said it's okay, I can stay all afternoon," Lori said as she hung up the phone. "Oh my gosh! I *love* those guys!" Lori had seen the posters and walked over to get a closer look.

"Me, too," I agreed. "But, now my heart belongs to him." I pointed to one of the posters.

Lori reached out to caress David Cassidy's image. "Yep," she agreed.

I put a *Partridge Family* Album on my record player for us to listen to while we talked. We discovered we both loved animals, swimming and being outdoors.

"Is having the darkest tan on the first day of school something you try to do?" I asked.

"Well, I freckle, but I would love to be tan, and my hair to be real blonde," Lori lifted a section of her hair, "instead of this dishwater color."

"I guess I'm lucky, I can get really dark." Remembering we came here to eat, I said, "Hey, let's go downstairs and make some lunch. Then, if you want, we could go out to the backyard and start working on our tans."

"Okay."

I kissed my cat and we headed downstairs to the kitchen. As we walked past my brother's room, we noticed he hadn't moved—Scott was engrossed with whatever he was building. I whispered to Lori, "I don't think he even noticed we're here."

In the kitchen, Lori and I grabbed the supplies out of the brown cabinets. I slapped together the peanut butter and jelly sandwiches on the bright orange countertop while Lori got some milk out of the brown refrigerator. "We can eat these over there," I said pointing to the white, round table in the breakfast room.

We ate quickly in silence and after we cleaned up, I said, "Ready to go outside?"

"Sure."

We opened the sliding glass door and stepped out to the patio, then looked around for the lounge chairs. We found them leaning against the house and dragged two out to the middle of the yard, between the house and a large old apple tree. We wanted to make sure the sunlight wasn't blocked by anything. After we'd positioned the chairs perfectly, we quickly doused our arms and legs with baby oil and sprawled across the chairs.

"You didn't mention it earlier, Bon, do you have any big plans this summer?" Lori asked.

"No, my dad can't take time off from work. What about you?"

"Same thing."

We sat silently for a few minutes.

"This is *b-o-r-i-n-g*!" I said. "I can't stand doing nothing. My mom usually reads when she's out here. She's so funny, she doesn't tan. Her goal is to make her freckles grow into each other so she looks tan. It doesn't work, but she keeps trying."

Lori laughed. "Your mom sounds nice."

"She's okay," I admitted. "What can we do while we're lying here?"

"I have an idea. Have you ever read the Bible?"

"No. Have you?"

"Just some of it—in church. I'm supposed to be reading sections from the New Testament of the Bible for my weekly catechism classes," Lori said.

"Ugh."

"Well, I want to read other parts as well, because my mom interprets it one way, my dad another, and the priest another. That makes me wonder who's right, if any of them, about the meanings of the Bible stories."

"That's a good point. My mom quotes things she says are in the 'Good Book' all the time. Things like 'Cleanliness is next to godliness, now go *clean* your room!' or 'Treat others as you would have them treat you, now be *nice* to your little brother!'" I said while shaking my finger at Lori. She chuckled. "It's Mom's way of telling me 'God is watching you!' We go to church almost every week. My mom listens to the minister, but my dad sleeps through the service, and my brother and I draw pictures or write stories in the margins of the program. I don't really listen, except when we sing. I love singing."

"How about we read the Bible out loud to each other and come up with our own interpretations? I bet it will take us all summer. Plus, you'd help make my catechism homework fun." Lori said.

"Yeah, I bet it'll take all summer. And, I guess it might be good to find out if all Mom's quotes are really in the Bible . . . that'd be great ammunition if they aren't! Okay, you've got a deal."

I went into the house and after wiping off the suntan oil from my hands, located my bible and my mother's Bible and brought them outside.

We spent every afternoon together that summer reading Bible stories. One week before our summer vacation ended, we finished reading the dark, strange verses in Revelation and closed the Bibles, deep in thought. We were very naive, as both of us had grown up in families that protected us from most of what went on in the world.

"What do you think that means?" Lori asked me. "It's like the *War of the Worlds*."

"Yeah, it is, isn't it? I don't really get all the symbolism of the four colored horses, serpents or any of it."

"I don't either. In time, I suppose we'll learn."

We sat in silence for a moment watching clouds pass by, then Lori said, "I think the world may end in our lifetime, and if not, for sure, in the next generation."

"I think you're right. I don't think it would be fair to bring kids into this world if they are just going to suffer and die."

That day we made a pact to each other never to have children.

2
CORRUPTION

That summer of innocence flew by. Our last week of freedom consisted of shopping with our parents for new school supplies and goofing off.

The summer sun had lightened our hair and kissed my skin a dark brown, while Lori's skin, despite her attempts to tan, only changed to a pale pink shade.

A few days before school started, Lori came over and we locked ourselves in my room and played a Bobby Sherman album so nobody could hear our conversation.

"Do you think high school will be fun?" Lori asked me as she sprawled across my bed on her stomach with her legs twisted up in the air behind her.

"I think so." I sat on a fuzzy pink rug with my legs stretched in front of me as I leaned back against the bed. "But I don't have older sisters, like you do. What have you heard?"

"Not much, except it's boring."

"Boring? How can it be boring? It's high school! I think it's going to be exciting. I really like going back to school in the fall and seeing everybody again. The only thing that scares me is it's so big and there will be a ton of kids I don't know coming from the other middle schools."

"I don't think my school will be like that. It'll be the same kids. My older sisters definitely don't think high school is *exciting.*" Lori said. "It's Catholic with nuns everywhere to whack our knuckles with rulers if we get out of line." We talked a little longer, before she had to go home for dinner.

After Labor Day weekend, we both entered high school. Lori attended her Catholic school while I spent my days at the new public high school.

My incoming freshman class would be the first class to graduate after attending the school all four years. Kids from several middle schools poured in from all socioeconomic backgrounds ranging from well-to-do to dire poverty.

I found myself at the most non-traditional school in the area. Even the architecture was non-traditional, consisting of several large circles constructed of red bricks connected by hallways to a middle circle. I always thought if I were to fly over the school and look down upon it, it would look like one of the 1960s love flowers found on VW Bugs. Instead of classrooms, four-foot-tall cubicle-style dividers segmented the large circles. Other schools in the area had older, seasoned teachers, but not at this school. The majority of the teachers had recently graduated from college, making them only four to seven years older than their students.

One day, shortly after school began, I took a shortcut to class by walking outside between two of the circles. A pungent, sickening sweet, odor assailed my nostrils. I looked around, wondering what and where that smell came from. Then I noticed a tall skinny guy wearing ripped jeans, a tee-shirt and a faded blue jean jacket leaning against the red brick wall. He stuck a fat cigarette in his mouth, slowly inhaled and held his breath.

How odd, I thought. My mother smoked, but her cigarettes didn't look like that, and she didn't hold the smoke in like he was doing either. "That's a funny smelling cigarette," I said approaching him. He looked down at me with bloodshot eyes and exhaled.

"It's a joint."

I had no idea what he meant by a joint. "Oh. What's in it?"

The guy looked at me like I was an idiot. "Pot."

"Pot?" I thought a pot was something you put flowers in.

"Yeah, pot, Mary Jane, weed, grass, marijuana. God, you're stupid."

I ignored his mean remark. "Marijuana? I thought that stuff was against the law. You shouldn't be smoking that."

The guy laughed. "Go away, little bitch."

Bitch, I thought to myself. I'd never heard that word either. I didn't like this guy. He was mean, so I hurried on to my class.

That afternoon when I got home from school, Mother stood in the kitchen in front of the stove, singing, while she prepared dinner.

"Mom, can I ask you something?"

As typical, she smiled and began with her, "You're an Ameri-*can*, you *can* do anything you put your mind to!" Keeping her eyes on the pork chops sizzling in the electric frying pan, she asked, "What is it, sweetie?"

"A guy called me a 'bitch' today. What does that mean?"

Mother dropped the metal spatula as she gasped and covered her mouth with her hand and looked at me wide-eyed. She quickly recovered, reaching for the spatula. "Who called you that?"

"Some guy at school. What's it mean?"

"It's a *bad* word," she said while giving me the 'I mean it!' look. "Don't ever say that word again!"

"Okay, but what does it mean?"

"It means a female dog."

"He called me a *dog*? Ooohhh, that guy *is* mean!"

"Yes, not the type of person you want to associate with," my mother said. "Now go change out of your school outfit, then come down and help me set the dinner table."

ଓଞ୍ଜ

The Nixon era was in full swing. Watergate break-in updates filled the front pages of newspapers across the nation. Broadcasts about flag burning in rebellion to the Vietnam War appeared nightly on the evening news with Walter Cronkite. Young men drafted to serve in 'Nam considered deserting to Canada, and flower children spoke about free love, burned bras and took psychedelic drugs regularly.

At school, I learned how isolated and protected I had been growing up. Boys wearing ski masks over their face—and nothing else—dashed through the cafeteria at lunchtime; fist fights broke out between boys over who-knows-what; young lovers skipped class to make out in the hallways; drugs—like mescaline, ThC and blotter acid were readily available throughout the school day; students smuggled alcohol into the football games and dances; and the young teachers granted A's to students who simply showed up for class—whether they were stoned or sober.

Attending this school gave me the ability to cross paths with people my parents never would have approved, but who intrigued me because their lifestyle was completely foreign to the world I knew. I quickly learned to censor what I shared with my parents about my school days. However, I burst with excitement waiting to share all of it with Lori on the weekends.

ଓଞ୍ଜ

Lori usually came over to my house, but one Saturday morning in early October, I rode my bike down the street to her house. The single-story, gray-brick ranch home had a black roof and black shutters around the front windows. A few small bushes surrounded the home, with one twenty-foot maple tree in front. The house looked rather ordinary, except for the inviting in-ground pool that took up most of the backyard.

Lori and I sat cross-legged facing each other on the bed in her room, which she shared with her older sister. It seemed every time we started to say something private, Marjorie came into the room to get something. We couldn't exactly kick her out.

"Let's go to your house, at least you have your own room," Lori said.

"Yeah, but I also have a brother. It wouldn't be any better."

"Okay, let's go for a walk . . . ," Lori looked at her sister who was searching for something in the closet, "so we can talk in private."

"I know. How about we take the tandem and ride out into the fields. Maybe we can find a place to talk somewhere."

"Yeah, a place without brothers or sisters!" Lori said as she got off the bed.

"Sounds good to me!"

The red and white built-for-two bicycle belonged to my parents, but they rarely rode it. Lori and I loved riding it, and since we weren't old enough to drive, we rode the tandem everywhere.

"Mom," I yelled in through the door from the garage, "Lori and I are going to take the tandem for a ride, okay?"

"Sure, sweetie, just be careful and be home when the streetlights come on," my mother called back from somewhere in the house.

"Your mom is so sweet, Bon," Lori said as we walked around my mother's car to move the bike out of the garage onto the driveway.

"She can be. But, when I'm in trouble and she yells, it's definitely *not* sweet."

Lori and I rode down the street to the dirt path leading into a field where new homes were supposed to be built in the next few years. For now, tall grass and some little weeping willow trees filled the field. We peddled over the trails in that field until we reached a busy road bordering our subdivision.

"Do you think there might be a good place on the other side of the road?" Lori said as she scanned the horizon.

"We won't know until we look. Let's go."

Cars were zooming past us at forty miles per hour from both directions on the two-lane road. We saw a break in traffic and prepared. Just before the last car flew by, I stood up over the front seat and Lori, who usually kicked her feet up on the back handlebars and enjoyed the ride, brought her feet down. Together we peddled as hard and fast as we could. Despite being honked at by two approaching cars and feeling the wind as they zoomed by, no brakes screeched and we made it across the road in one piece. After reaching safety, we stopped a moment to scan the area.

"Hey, there's a trail leading over to that big field," I said pointing it out. "Wanna check it out?"

"Sure."

We followed the dirt path. The field had several small hills, a few large elm and maple trees and dozens of trails leading all over it. I slowed the bike down and then planted one leg on the ground and Lori did the same.

"Lori, do you see that big old tree over there?" I asked her as I pointed it out.

"Which one?"

"The really fat one with all those leaves and branches that looks like an open umbrella. Do you see it?"

"Yeah."

"Let's go check that out. It looks like it might be a great place to hang out."

Lori agreed and off we rode. We got off the bike and rested it against the trunk. The foliage-filled branches blocked the sunlight and prevented grass from growing beneath the tree.

"This is huge! Let's see if we can wrap our arms around the trunk."

I giggled, "Oh, so you're a tree hugger, eh?"

"No," she said as she walked around to the other side. "I just bet we can't even reach each other's hands." Lori was right. We couldn't. The trunk was huge. "This tree must be a hundred years old."

"Or older."

Lori came back around and together we sat on the soft dirt surrounding the trunk's base and leaned back against the tree.

"This is the perfect spot!" Lori said as she stood back up and twirled around. "We can see all around us, yet, these small bushes hide us from sight if we don't want to be found." Lori stopped spinning and looked directly at me. "This is a *perfect* place—our 'Umbrella Tree'!"

I agreed. Lori sat back down next to me and looked out over the small hills.

"Lor, have you ever heard the word, 'bitch'?"

"Yeah, my sisters call each other that all the time, when they're fighting."

"Really? But do you know what it means?"

Lori looked at me for a moment, then back out to the field. "No, not really. I just figure it's not nice."

"It means female dog."

Lori started laughing. "That's great. My sisters are calling each other dogs. That's funny!" Lori smothered her giggles and then said, "Why did you ask?"

"Oh this guy at school called me that. He's a real loser."

"Why did he call you that? Did you do something?"

"Well, he was smoking this really weird looking cigarette and I asked him what it was. He told me a marijuana cigarette; he called it a joint."

Lori turned fully toward me. "Wait a minute, you're telling me this kid was smoking dope on campus during school?"

"Yep."

"Wow, your school *is* different."

Before I could respond, we both heard a low-pitched rumbling noise.

"What's that?" I asked.

"Don't know. Sounds like an engine or . . ." Three boys riding mini-bikes crested over one of the small hills in the distance. "*BOYS!*"

For the next hour or so, Lori and I stayed under the cover of the "umbrella tree" watching those daredevils. The boys practiced all kinds of stunts, jumps, spins and other racing maneuvers never realizing they had an audience. It amazed us that they didn't get hurt.

From that day on, whenever Lori and I got together, we'd walk or ride the tandem to "our tree" in "our field." I continued sharing with her what kids were doing at my "anything goes" high school. Lori listened and always seemed amazed and told me nothing exciting ever happened at her school.

"Hey Lor, you know that song *Love The One You're With* by Stephen Stills?" I asked her one day as we settled under the tree.

Lori sang one line of the song. "Yeah, I know it."

"Well, I hear it's the motto for the slut society at school. These girls, there's about a dozen of them, walk around singing it, and then they do it—seriously, go from one guy to the next!"

Lori's eyes grew large, "No!"

"Yeah! These eleventh and twelfth grade girls. I bet some of them get pregnant . . . and then I wonder if they'll still be living their lives based on that song's advice."

"They'll learn. Hey, did you hear about that lawsuit trying to get abortion legal?" Lori asked.

"Nope."

Lori told me about some lawyers in Texas fighting to change the law because girls were bleeding to death from botched abortions in back alleys.

"Do you think abortions should be legal?" I asked her. "I mean you *are* going to a Catholic school. Aren't you against abortions?"

Lori didn't even hesitate. "It depends. I don't think the government should be involved. It's a personal decision." She had obviously given this some serious thought. "The decision should be the girl's or woman's, and if there's a man still in the picture, he should be involved too. Ultimately, it's her body, and she's the one who will have to deal with her choice every day of her life."

CR80

Each weekend I always had something to share with Lori. Going to that school was like being on the set of a soap opera. One week I'd tell Lori about how the teachers were smoking dope, drinking and hanging out with students; the next it would be about the school football game and dance—and the kids that got sick from drinking and/or drugs.

"Guess what happened this week!" I teased Lori.

"Oh, let's see. A fight?" I shook my head. "I know, one of the teachers got high with a bunch of students." I shook my head again. "Okay, last guess, one of the slut society members is pregnant."

"Nope. The jocks on the student council got real mad at the freak group, because the freaks are always smoking in the bathrooms and then the smell goes all over the school, and the jocks think it's gross. So, the council put together a proposal that *everybody* liked and signed and presented it to the school principal and administrator—and now our school has an 'official smoking area.' Pretty cool, huh?"

Lori's eyes became as round as saucers. "Wow, the school is letting the students smoke?"

"Yeah. I guess they figured there was no use trying to get the kids not to smoke at school, so instead they set up this area with benches and ashtrays between two of the circles for the smokers to go do their thing."

"Wow. That has got to be a first."

"The thing is, a lot of my school friends smoke, so I won't see them near as much, unless I go out there. It's the cool place to be now. I guess that backfired on the jocks who thought they were the cool ones."

CR80

Lori and I both wanted to shed our "sweet, good girl" reputations so boys would notice us. Within a year's time, we had changed. My mother insisted that I wear dresses to school, but I wanted to fit in so I began keeping secrets from her. I would go to school in a dress; however, once there, I'd immediately change to some hip hugger, elephant-bell blue jeans I kept stashed in my locker.

Lori and I also started smoking cigarettes because we thought that would make us "cool." We figured both of our mothers smoked, so they probably wouldn't notice it anyway. Plus, if we had cigarettes to offer to the boys, that gave us a reason to talk to them, and then the boys would start noticing us.

Every weekend we'd ride the tandem over to the field, get off the bike, lean it against "our tree," and then roll up our blue jeans to remove the cigarettes we'd hidden in our knee socks. After lighting up, we'd walk outside the shade of the "umbrella tree," hoping to find the boys. Sometimes we did, sometimes we didn't . . . but we always had fun. That field became our meeting place to smoke, watch the boys, gossip about kids at school and share lessons of life.

3
OUR ALIBI

One hot Saturday afternoon during the summer of 1973, Lori and I rode the tandem toward the nearby 7-11. We purposely took the long way winding through the neighborhoods to avoid the busy streets. Before leaving, both of us carefully hid a single cigarette under our anklet socks. Shortly before reaching 7-11, we stopped and lit up our smokes, which were now a little damp from our sweat. As we both drew our first drag, Lori heard a car and looked around and shouted, "Your *MOM!*"

I looked over my shoulder in disbelief, but sure enough, my mother, a petite woman with short, curly, reddish-brown hair and big golden-brown eyes, sat behind the steering wheel slowly driving up the street in the 1963 black Chevy Nova Super Sport my father had surprised her with for her birthday several years earlier. *Why would she be driving up this street?* I had no idea.

"Oh no!" I stomped out my only cigarette with my foot. Even though Mother smoked, I knew I'd be in huge trouble if she caught me.

Lori did the same then we both popped some mints into our mouths to hide the tobacco smell.

Mother pulled up beside us with a huge smile that lit up her face. "What a surprise to see you girls here. Where are you heading?"

I gulped down the guilt and answered, "Oh, we're just going to 7-11 to get a Slurpee."

"Okay, well, you girls have fun. It's a beautiful day, just be sure you are home by the time the streetlights come on, sweetie." We watched her drive away down the street.

Once she turned the corner and disappeared from our sight, Lori exhaled a sigh of relief. "Wow! That was a close one!"

"Yeah, I wonder if she suspected anything," I said as we stood there straddling the bike on the side of the road.

"I don't think so," Lori said, "but now our cigarettes are gone."

"I wonder where she was going? I was so scared of getting caught smoking, I forgot to ask. I guess it doesn't matter."

"Probably the grocery store," Lori said. "Hey, how about we head over to the Alibi? Maybe we can bum a smoke from someone there."

"Hey, that sounds fun!"

The Alibi, a little hole-in-the-wall pool hall for teenagers, occupied the lot catty-corner behind 7-11. When we stepped inside, the air-conditioned coolness greeted us. We stood framed in the doorway for a moment to give our eyes time to adjust from the bright afternoon sunshine to the dim lighting inside. Several pool tables filled the open space. Near the front, a jukebox played some rock music and a vending machine stood in the back of the room. Fluorescent green paint camouflaged the cement block walls and rock star posters hung on the walls and dangled from the ceiling. The Alibi provided the only place of its kind for kids between sixteen and eighteen. Although the staff prohibited alcohol on the premises, nobody said anything about smoking.

The only people inside were two guys playing pool and the attendant. We didn't recognize the pool players. They were older than us, dressed in jeans and tee-shirts, and both had brown hair cascading several inches below their shoulders. Lori sauntered over to them. One had a cigarette hanging out of his mouth. He leaned over the table, aimed and took his shot, knocking two balls into opposite pockets. He straightened up, not noticing Lori behind him.

"Excuse me," she said. "I'm hoping I could bum a cigarette from you?"

The guy turned toward Lori and looked her up and down. That day both of us wore cut-off denim shorts along with red bandana halter-tops we had made ourselves out of large handkerchiefs. As the guy's eyes came back up to meet Lori's, he smiled.

"Sure," he said as he motioned to his friend to give her a cigarette.

"Any chance I could have two—one for my friend over there?" Lori pointed at me standing near the jukebox across the room.

Both guys looked me up and down, just as they had Lori, and smiled. I could feel a rush of heat radiating from my face, which I knew matched the shade of my halter top. I tried to act nonchalant and smiled back.

"Sure." Speaking loud enough for me to hear, the pool player asked Lori, "So what's your name? Where are you girls from?"

"Lori. That's Bonny," Lori said nodding her head in my direction. "We live a few miles away."

The three talked for a few minutes at a lower volume, then Lori walked back over to me and whispered, "Aren't they cute?" as she handed me a cigarette.

"Yeah, but Lor, they seem w-a-y older than we are, don't you think?"

"What's wrong with that?" she asked as she lit her cigarette.

I lit my cigarette off Lori's. Something about those guys made me nervous. They obviously were not the type of boys

---

I'd ever take home to meet Mother. They were what she'd categorize as "bad boys." Curiosity got the better of me. "What did they say to you?"

"Not much." Lori didn't seem too enthralled with them any longer. "Let's play some music," she suggested stepping around me to look at the selection on the Jukebox. "Oh, here's one!" She slid in a quarter, and the room quickly filled with loud music from Black Sabbath.

"*Ironman*! I love that song!" I yelled above the music. Lori and I both sang along at full volume.

The Alibi soon became "our place" and *Ironman* became "our song." Over the next few years, each time we walked into the building, we went straight to the jukebox, slid a quarter in to play "our song" then selected pool sticks from the rack on the wall while singing at the top of our lungs.

Neither of us liked being in crowded places. Rarely did the Alibi become so crammed we felt claustrophobic. And, of course, rarely did other girls come into the pool hall. We liked it that way. The guys flirted with us, but we knew we were safe in their company. For the next few years, if we weren't at home or in the field under "our tree," we could be found at the Alibi, flirting with the boys, playing pool, singing *Ironman* and smoking cigarettes.

4
TRAGEDY

When we could, Lori and I spent the weekends together throughout our sophomore year of high school. During the weekdays, however, we were making new friends at our respective high schools. Unfortunately, my parents, especially my mother, didn't approve of my new "rowdy crowd" friends. To keep me away from them, my parents constantly found reasons to ground me, and it seemed I got into trouble more often than not. Being grounded meant even Lori, who wasn't rowdy, couldn't come over to visit or even talk to me on the phone. As a result, Lori found other things to do on the weekends and we started drifting apart.

My mother, who had done her best to provide my brother and me with an idealistic childhood, was beside herself not knowing how to keep me sheltered from experiencing the corruption of the 1970s—a world of drugs, free love and experimentation. She worried endlessly, resulting in her suffering a severe asthma attack. Father rushed her to the hospital where the doctors performed a tracheotomy and put her on cortisone. The doctors warned her to limit her intake of the medication because eventually her body could build up a resistance to the cortisone and then it would no longer work.

Because I was still a minor, hospital rules prevented me from visiting Mother on my own and my father didn't want me to see her in a hospital bed, so I had to wait until she returned home to talk privately with her.

"Mom, I'm sorry I caused you so much worry."

My mother reached out to hug me. I went into her arms, careful not to disrupt the gauze bandage covering the hole in her throat. "Honey, I'm a natural-born worrier. I just want you to have a good life and enjoy the finer things life offers. Those friends of yours are heading to the dark side, and I don't want them to take you there."

Having been sheltered for so long, I really didn't understand what Mother was referring to. I just wanted to have fun.

"Hey Mom, did you notice?" I said as I smiled revealing my straight pearly whites. While mother had been hospitalized, after three years of being a "metal mouth," my braces had finally been removed.

"Beautiful smile!"

"Thanks, Mom. Are you feeling okay now?" I asked looking her in the eyes.

"Yes. But, quite honestly, I don't think I will be able to survive another attack."

"Mom! Don't say that! Please. We need you! You've got to fight!"

"I'm tired, sweetie," Mother said with a sad smile on her face. I wasn't quite sure if she meant she wanted to take a nap "tired" or too "tired" to fight her illness. Changing the subject, she asked, "Is your homework done?"

I left her to go do my schoolwork, not really understanding Mother's last comment.

For the next several months Mother was the poster child of good health. Her energy was up, she was active and doing a million things at once. Her haunting prediction faded to the back of my mind.

CRℰSO

Early in my junior year, I started going steady with Andrew. He stood eight inches taller than I, had shoulder-length light-blond hair and big blue eyes. We had the same sense of humor and always had fun together. He lived in a yellow farmhouse directly across the street from our high school, so we usually spent our lunch hours at his house during the week. If I was not working at the ice cream parlor or grounded, on the weekends, I spent most of my spare time with Andrew, rather than Lori.

That changed suddenly in November of 1974.

The Saturday prior to Thanksgiving, a humid cold front blew into Saginaw Valley causing Mother's asthma to flare up. By the next day, she fought for each breath. Father had brought home a large, heavy oxygen tank and settled her into the study downstairs. The mask supplying her oxygen left only her eyes and forehead exposed.

I stood at the bottom of the stairs as Father walked out of the study, looking down, massaging his forehead with his hand. "Dad?" He dropped his hand and looked up. Father had a dark complexion, thick, jet-black hair, and stormy dark eyes. However, as I looked at him now, I noticed dread had replaced the storm in his eyes.

"Bonny, I don't think the oxygen is working and I don't want to wait for an ambulance, so I'm going to pack her overnight bag and take your mother to the hospital." As Father started up the stairs to their bedroom he said over his shoulder, "Please go in there and remove her fingernail polish. Her doctor always wants to see if her nails have a pink or blue tint when she first comes in."

I had feared my father for the last several years. Whenever he talked to me, especially after I started hanging out with my rowdy friends, he'd bark at me. Just a few weeks earlier, he had thrown me over his lap and swatted me with his belt because I had come home late.

"You can't spank me, I'm a teenager!" I screamed in rebellion.

While the belt slapped the skin on the back of my thighs, he responded in a deadly quiet voice, "I can and will. You are a disgrace to this family. As far as I'm concerned, you are dead."

My mother had been standing there, crying and quickly came to my defense, but his words were out. They stabbed my heart. It seemed nothing I ever did met with his approval. He never encouraged me, hugged me or said he loved me.

Mother was quite the opposite. She always encouraged me. Always asked about my day. Always seemed interested. Always took the time to listen. I had no doubt in my mind that Mother loved me. I couldn't say the same about Father.

He had never been a worrier. Around Mother, Father behaved like a happy-go-lucky boy, the jokester, the prankster. He could make Mother laugh until she cried or "had an accident," or make her so angry she'd lock herself in the closet and scream "Oh *SUGAR!*" at the top of her lungs and then open the door to step out as if all was right with the world. Mother's emotions ran the gamut with Father in her life.

But now, he seemed really worried. I could see it in his deep-brown eyes. I went upstairs into the bathroom, grabbed some fingernail polish remover, some cotton balls then hurried back downstairs to Mother. She held herself up on the edge of the couch with her arms. Despite having the oxygen mask covering her face, she sucked in air loudly, fighting for each breath she inhaled. Mother lifted her head to look up at me as I walked in.

"Hi, Mom. Dad told me to take your fingernail polish off," I said as I knelt down on the floor in front of the couch. Mother nodded and held out her left hand. As I touched it, a very strange vibration shot up my arm. It surprised me. I looked up into my mother's hazel eyes. She attempted to smile as if to say, "I love you."

"Don't talk, Mom, save your breath." I looked down at the soft hand I held. Looking at her perfectly manicured nails, the dimples at the base of her fingers, the shining diamond ring and wedding band she treasured. Unexpected tears filled my eyes, nearly blinding me from completing my task.

As I finished removing the polish, Father walked in with Mother's small suitcase. He set it down and then carried the oxygen tank out and placed it in the back seat of the car. "Are you ready, Louise?" he asked as he reentered the room. Mother nodded. I watched as my father lovingly picked up and cradled the woman he'd married twenty-three years earlier. He kissed her forehead and quickly carried her to the car waiting in the driveway. I followed and put the overnight bag in the backseat while Father adjusted the mask back over Mother's nose and mouth then quickly sat in the driver's seat and backed the car down the driveway. I watched silently from the front yard with tears streaming down my face as Father raced Mother away to the hospital.

I went to my bedroom and nuzzled my cat for companionship. I had never seen Father this unsettled. Would Mother survive this attack or would her premonition come true?

A little past six the next morning, the phone rang beside my bed and jarred me awake. Throwing back the pink comforter my mother had recently made, I grabbed the receiver. "Hello?" A nurse from the hospital asked to speak to my father.

I spurted out, "What's wrong?"

"I need to speak with your father," the nurse insisted.

Father picked up the other extension, but I continued to listen. "Your wife has taken a turn for the worse; you need to come right away."

I ran to my brother's bedroom and shook him for several minutes, it seemed, before he woke up. Then I quickly dressed and flew downstairs, taking two stairs at a time. Father stood at the closet yanking his overcoat off the hanger.

"Dad?"

Father threw on the coat and grabbed his keys. "Take your mother's car and drive your brother and yourself to school. I've got to get to the hospital."

"Dad?" I said again.

My father turned to me with an agitated look and snapped, "What?"

"Is she going to be okay?"

"I don't know. I'm leaving. Go to school," he ordered as he raced out to the garage. A few moments later, I heard the tires squeal as he drove off.

A very strange numbness slowly spread throughout my body. Something felt wrong—really wrong.

During my third period shorthand class, the PA system came to life with a static crackle. A second later a female voice announced, "Scott and Bonny Brookes please report to the office."

"Oh no. Mom!" I said aloud as I quickly scooped up and clutched my books to my chest. Everyone in class looked at me, but I didn't care. I ran to the office and arrived before my brother. The secretary asked me if I knew my mother was sick. *Duh.* "Yes," I paused. "What happened?"

"Your father called and said you and your brother are to go home immediately . . . that's all I know," she said avoiding my eyes. I wondered why she wouldn't look at me. I knew she knew something, but wouldn't tell me.

I impatiently waited for my younger brother, keeping watch through the office window toward the locker area. Finally he arrived. "We need to go home." I led the way out of the office. He followed in silence as we walked through the parking lot to Mother's Chevy Nova.

We got in, not looking at each other. I turned the key and the engine roared to life. "If she's dead," he said while looking out the passenger window, "it's your fault, and I'll never forgive you." Wow, Scott's words hurt, yet I understood and already felt guilty. I had caused Mother to stress out, bringing on the asthma.

I brought the car to a stop in our driveway and the garage door rose. Our father stood with his arms outstretched and rivers of tears flowing down his face. I had never seen him cry. "Mama's gone," he softly said, wrapping his arms around both of us.

I was stunned, but not surprised. Mother had told me a year earlier and I knew it when I touched her hand the day before. "When did she die? What caused it?" I asked my father.

"When the call came through this morning, she had already passed. They didn't want to tell me over the phone. The cortisone stopped working, and so did her heart." At forty-two, Mother's time on earth had come to an end.

My brother and I stood there in Father's arms for a few minutes; each of us lost in our private thoughts.

I broke the silence. "Dad?"

"Yes?"

"If Mom had already died by six this morning, why weren't we called from school until eleven?"

My father looked down at me. "I needed time to myself first, and then I called your mother's parents, and my parents, and then I called the school, and then our nearest neighbors. Some are inside waiting for us. Let's go in now," my father said before guiding us to the door through the garage.

Several neighbors and friends of my parents sat or stood in our living room. All there to give support to Father. One by one, they came up to give me a hug and say, "I'm sorry." I got so sick of hearing that! What do they have to be sorry about? They didn't kill her. I tried to be civil, but I couldn't portray the "I'm okay" facade much longer.

I went into the kitchen to get some water. I filled the glass then set it down, semi-consciously realizing I had no thirst. Glancing up, I noticed the clock through my fog. Three o'clock. Lori would be home from school.

I walked like a zombie up the stairs to my room closing the door behind me to block out the low muffle of voices drifting up from downstairs. Thomasina slept on my bed. I absentmindedly petted her with one hand while I dialed Lori's number with the other. Within minutes, she sat at my side with her arm wrapped around me as I rested my head on her shoulder and cried.

She continued to hold me as she reminded me how much my mother loved me. Lori wanted to fix things, make things right. So, in true "Lori fashion," she reminded me of the funny things Mother did. "Your mom was so cute. The way she'd check on you before you left the house." Lori did her best imitation of my mother's upbeat, energetic voice. "Now did you brush your hair and comb your teeth? No, no, I mean comb your teeth and brush your hair? No, no, well, you know what I mean!" We both laughed through the tears.

Lori continued talking as I fought to get my sobbing under control. She reminded me about when Mother came so close to catching us doing our naughty things, like smoking. Lori acted as the anchor in my turbulent sea of emotions.

Andrew came by shortly afterwards, and the three of us went outside, for a walk and to smoke some cigarettes. My mother now resided in heaven. That stark reality was a hard pill for me to swallow.

CRSO

The morning of Mother's funeral, I remembered I had been scheduled to go into work at the ice cream parlor that evening. "This is Bonny, and I'm calling to let you know I can't come in tonight."

"You can't come in today? It's one of the busiest days of the year, no excuses are accepted. You be here for your shift, or you won't have a job," the manager said.

"My mom died, her funeral is today—"

"Now I've heard lots of excuses today from you kids," the chain-smoking female manager said in her raspy voice, "but I'm not falling for any of them. Plus, you should know that your excuse can be checked out."

The minimum wage job was a joke. I spent the majority of my time scooping ice cream or cleaning up melted messes from the little kids who knocked their scoops off their cones to the floor. "So you're calling me a liar. Nice to know you think so highly of me," I said sarcastically. I really didn't have any energy or desire to fight for my job. "Well, do whatever. I won't be there," I said and hung up.

This isn't happening, I kept thinking to myself as I dressed in my black mini dress, black nylons and black platform heels in preparation for the funeral. *It's just a bad nightmare.* But, unfortunately, my mother's death was all too real. Soon I climbed in the car to join my father and brother and we drove in silence to the funeral home to say goodbye to the most important woman in each of our lives.

Mourners packed in at Mother's service the day before Thanksgiving. Her life had touched so many. They had all loved her. I loved her too. I felt numb and lost among all these strangers. Thankfully, I had Lori there to lean on.

5
ON OUR OWN

After Mother passed away, my family fell apart. Father was rarely home: Either because of work—he started teaching insurance classes at night, in addition to his day job—or, maybe, because being home was just too hard. I didn't know. At any rate, our close-knit family unraveled without Mother there to keep us tied together. Realization dawned on me that she had been the hub, with my father, brother and myself as the spokes of our family wheel. With her missing, the family dinners; family drives; encouragement, love and support had vanished. Instead, the environment changed to one of "fend for yourself."

Near the end of the summer, Father took a short trip and left his credit card with me, along with instructions to take care of my little brother. I did as he asked and purchased the food and school clothes consisting of pants, shirts, skirts, socks and shoes. However, the next month when the credit card statement arrived, he went ballistic. He yelled and screamed and swore at me while waving the statement in the air. After his tirade, he grounded me—again.

I went up to my room, climbed on my bed, wrapped my arms around Thomasina and cried into her fur. She purred and licked the tears off my face. At least she loved me. In Father's eyes, I could never do anything right. All I ever wanted was for him to be proud of me. Yet once again, I had justified his disappointment in me.

After he left that night to teach his class, I called Lori. I knew I was grounded and not supposed to be on the phone, but my brother stayed locked in his room and I figured he wouldn't be the wiser if I muffled my voice by playing my Pink Floyd *Dark Side of the Moon* album.

"Lori, I'm miserable. My dad grounded me."

"Oh, Bon." Lori said. "Why? What happened?"

I told her about the credit card.

"That seems a little irrational. I mean he did tell you to take care of you and your brother."

"That's what I thought. I don't know why my dad doesn't love me."

"He does, Bon."

"I can see the sadness and loneliness in his eyes. I know he feels cheated out of years of life with Mom. But, what about my feelings?"

"Bon, you've got to give him time." She was right. I was too wrapped up in my feelings to think about his. "Are you sure something else is not going on?" Lori asked.

"Well, I think he's moving on; I think he met someone."

"Really?"

"Yeah, a student in his class. I've only met her once, but he's gone so much, it can't all be for work."

"What's she like?"

I brought up a mental image of the woman. "She looks like Dolly Parton with curves and thick, long platinum blonde hair, big blue eyes and dimples."

"Okay, so she's pretty, but what is she like? Do you like her?"

I thought a moment before answering. "She seems nice enough. But she's definitely not anything like Mom. Plus she's only fifteen years older than I am and eleven years younger than Dad. I think she may be after my father for his money, rather than him. Despite how hurt and how angry my dad makes me, Mom's death shattered his heart and I don't want him to get hurt again."

"Bon, it's your dad's life. Let him live it."

"Yeah, okay. So, my dad is moving on with his life; and that's why I'm thinking I want to move on with mine." I told Lori my idea.

"And you think moving out is the answer?"

"Yes."

"I thought you lost your job at the ice cream place. Did you find another job, you didn't tell me about?"

"I did lose that job but they called me back after they saw Mom's obituary to apologize and offer it back, but I have no desire to be around people whose opinion of me is so low. I deal with enough of that at home."

"So, did you get another job?"

"No."

"Well, you need a job."

"I'll find one."

Lori paused. "Okay, but what about high school? Are you going to drop out?"

"No, I'll finish. But, I'll be eighteen in a few weeks and I don't think there's anything Dad can do to prevent me from leaving at that point. Hell, I think he'd love for me to leave," I said as a few tears escaped from the corners of my eyes. "I miss Mom."

Lori's compassion rang through her voice. "I know you do. I'd come down there, but I don't want you to get in more trouble."

"Yeah, that wouldn't be cool. I guess I'd better go before my brother discovers I'm on the phone."

The following Monday, I stopped at the library after school to check into the law about leaving home before I graduated from high school. After learning I could, excitement bubbled inside me as I began dreaming about having my own place.

CR&D

In celebration of my eighteenth birthday, the legal drinking age, Andrew took me to a popular nightclub. At least *he* remembered. I loved orange juice, so he bought me a mimosa. People laughed, smoked, drank, danced and fell over each other inside the bar. Several patrons collapsed into me as they tried to make their way on and off the dance floor. After being knocked into for the umpteenth time, I turned to grab my purse hanging on the back of my chair, but it wasn't there. Andrew and I looked all around us, with no luck. I went into the girl's bathroom. There sat my purse on top of the trash bin. My wallet and my asthma inhaler were gone. Terrific.

I just wanted to get out of there. I went back to Andrew, dangling my purse on my fingers.

"You found it!"

"Yeah, but my wallet and asthma inhaler are gone."

"Somebody probably thought your inhaler was a bong."

"Great." I looked at Andrew with misery in my eyes. "I want to go home." Always the gentleman, Andrew granted my wish.

That night I sat in my room, alone and lonely. Thomasina, as always, sat at my side. Yet I felt so terribly unloved by my remaining family. I couldn't handle it. It was glaringly obvious to me how unwanted I was in that household. I saw no point in living there any longer. I would finish high school, because Mother would have wanted me to, but the time to move out had come. All I needed was a job and a plan. The next afternoon I called Lori.

"Hey, wanna go for a ride?"

"Sure, where are we going?"

"Nowhere in particular. I just want to talk."

"Okay. I'm ready whenever you are," Lori said.

Within minutes, she climbed into the red leather passenger seat of the Chevy Nova and for the next hour we drove around the country roads that surrounded our town.

"Remember when I told you I wanted to move out?" I asked Lori. She nodded. "Well, I'm going to do it, but I need a job first. Do you think your dad would hire me at the drugstore?"

She took out a cigarette from her purse and lit up. I asked her to light a smoke for me too.

"Sorry, Bon, but there aren't any openings." Lori paused to light me a cigarette. "You know . . ."

"Know what?"

"I saw a help wanted sign at our old 7-11 the other day. You should check that out."

"Yeah? Thanks, Lor!" a small seed of enthusiasm began to grow within me.

The next day I drove Mother's car over to the nearby convenience store. As I put the car in park, I saw the sign taped in the window. I turned off the car, closed my eyes and sat for a moment to fight the nervousness I felt churning inside me. The memory of that day with Lori on the tandem flashed in my mind. I smiled, then took a deep breath and went inside to apply for the cashier's job.

The owner hired me to work the four to eleven shift—a perfect arrangement that allowed me to continue going to school. I began to see my escape route. Four days later, I started working at 7-11.

Over the next few weeks, I scanned the local paper for rooms for rent. Soon I found the perfect place—a white craftsman-styled house built during the 1920s. It had recently been converted into two apartments. The upstairs apartment consisted of a living room, a kitchen, small bath and a decent sized bedroom. The house faced a busy street, but being only ten blocks or so from work, the location worked. With my wages from 7-11, I could easily pay the rent, and thankfully, I had inherited Mother's car, so getting to and from work and school presented no problem. After I signed the six-month lease, I headed home to box up my belongings.

When my father walked in the door that evening, I timidly said, "Dad?"

He didn't look at me as he sat down and picked up the paper, opening to the business section. "Yes?"

"Ah, Dad, I'm going to move out."

Father folded the paper and looked at me. "You are?"

I had his full attention. "Yes. As you know, I have a full-time job and I've found an apartment." Father kept his eyes on me as he listened. "Don't worry, though, I'm going to finish school and plan on going to college in the fall. I signed a six-month lease today."

When I finished, he got off the couch and approached me. My nerves tingled because I didn't know how he'd react. "I think you'll be just fine," he said. "You can come home to do your laundry and I'll pay the car insurance to help you out."

Wow. That was easy. All that trepidation for nothing. "Okay . . . can I bring Thomasina with me?"

Father thought about it for a moment. "No, I don't think that's a good idea. She's twelve years old now, and I don't think it would be good for her. You can come back here anytime to visit."

"Oh, okay." My heart sank, but I understood.

"I'm proud of you for venturing out on your own."

Wow! He was proud of me? That meant the world to me. "You are?"

"Yes. When are you moving? I'll help you pack."

He'll help me pack? I thought. *Maybe Father was just eager to get rid of me. Did he really mean, 'Don't let the door hit you on the way out?' Perhaps my initial feelings about not being wanted there were correct after all.* Either way, he did help me pack and within a week, I had settled into my new home . . . and the next chapter of my life.

Lori came over to the apartment every weekend. When we first tried beer, it tasted disgusting, almost like drinking soap. But, maybe, the cheap brand we initially tried had something to do with that. We tasted another brand. Not so bad. It soon became the weekend routine for me to finish working at eleven at night, buy some beer, then head to my apartment where Lori and several other friends waited for me. We'd stay up until the wee hours of the morning drinking, smoking and talking.

Those were the crazy days! On the weekends, we'd party until sunrise sometimes. During the week, I woke up at six to get to school on time, then on to 7-11 to work until eleven, then do homework or housecleaning until my energy level wound down, usually around one or two in the morning. I never seemed to sleep, yet managed to keep my job, and do well in school.

One early Saturday morning, after a few beers, Lori told me she was going to drop out of school.

"Why? We're seniors! It's only a few months and we'll be done!"

Lori studied the beer in her hand, wiping off the condensation from the can before looking up at me. "Because, school is a bore."

I knew there had to be another reason. "Is that all?"

Lori chugged the rest of her beer and then walked into the kitchen to throw the can away. I followed her.

"Lor? What aren't you telling me?"

She leaned back against the counter top and quickly glanced at me before diverting her eyes downward. "My grades suck and I don't think I'll graduate this year. It's just better I drop out."

I watched Lori as she stared at the floor for a few moments. "What do your parents say?"

"They don't care."

Though both of her parents worked long hours and were rarely home, I couldn't believe they were okay with her dropping out. "Really?"

"Yeah." Lori looked up. "I need a smoke." She walked back to the living room.

"Lor," I said as I trailed behind her, "How about you transfer to my school? You need your diploma. I think you'd like it, I could help you, and we could see each other a lot more. Plus, it's an easy school to get through."

With each reason I gave her for transferring, Lori shook her head more vehemently. "My mind's made up."

I knew at that point there was nothing I could say to convince her otherwise and I didn't want to ruin a great friendship, so I let it go. "Well, I care about you, Lor, and just don't want you to do something you're going to regret later."

Lori snuffed out her cigarette in the ashtray and looked directly at me. "I won't."

Lori dropped out later that week and a few months later I graduated from high school with nearly straight A's.

6
THE PARK

At eighteen, we thought we knew it all, including that our lives were going to change very soon. The summer before I entered college, Lori and I hung out every day. We wanted to make as many memories as possible that summer . . . and so we did.

Like the summer day we went to a park with a small lake to party with the boys. A huge sign prohibiting alcohol greeted park visitors. Drinking beer would be too obvious, so Lori and I had an idea. We dropped by "our" 7-11 to buy a couple of 7-Up Slurpees. Then we headed over to the nearby liquor store where we purchased a pint of sloe gin.

On the way to the park, Lori reached over to turn up the volume on the radio. "I love this song," she said.

I had heard it before, but didn't really know it. Lori started singing, "Love, Love will keep us together . . ." After listening to the chorus of the new single by *The Captain and Tennille*, I joined in and began harmonizing with Lori. Our voices sounded great together! *Love Will Keep Us Together* became our "other song," because we knew, no matter what, we'd always be friends.

When we arrived at the park, the boys weren't there yet. Not a cloud could be found in the sky, and the sun's rays beat down on us. We decided not to wait for the boys before indulging in our cold drinks. We poured some sloe gin into our 7-Up Slurpees then blended the red liquid in with our straws. They tasted great!

Leaning against the car, sipping our frozen drinks, we looked at the smooth refreshing blue water of the lake.

"It sure is hot out." Lori swiped some sweat off her forehead with the back of her hand. "And, that water sure looks good."

"Yeah, it does," I said. "Too bad, we didn't wear our bikinis under our clothes."

Lori turned to me with a mischievous grin on her face. "We don't need bikinis, let's go skinny dipping!"

"Oh, Lori. *No!*" I had never skinny dipped in my life and I certainly wasn't going to start now.

"Why not? Are you chicken?" Lori put her hands up under her armpits and flapped her arms.

"Cut it out," I said turning away from her. "It's just I don't relish the idea of being naked outside, especially with the boys coming any minute."

"Who knows when they will get here. It's just for a few minutes so we can cool off. Real quick dip. We can go over by those trees, where nobody can see us. Come on!" Lori said and took off running toward the trees. Reluctantly, I followed.

Within moments, we stood at the edge of the lake behind the cover of some bushes and removed our cut-off denim shorts, tank tops and underwear before quickly slipping into the water. I squatted to cover my nakedness as I made my way out to deeper water. Not Lori, she didn't seem to have any modesty as she strutted out. When we reached a spot where we had a good view of the parking lot and where the lake water covered us up to our shoulders, we stopped and took a sip of our "Sloe Slurpees" and then carefully held them above the water.

"Doesn't this feel great?" Lori said.

I felt very awkward being naked outside, but Lori was right. "Yeah, it *does* feel good."

We had been in the cool water for less than three minutes when we heard the noise of an engine in the distance. "Someone's coming!" Adrenalin rushed through me as I looked back to shore and wondered if I'd be able to get there in time. Focusing on our garments heaped in a small pile, I held my drink high in the air as I started running in slow motion toward land through the chest-high, then waist-high, then thigh-high water.

Lori pointed, "The guys are here."

My eyes followed her finger to see three boys climb out of a pick-up truck's cab and three more boys jump out of the truck's bed. They had seen my car. "Oh my God, run!"

Lori laughed as the water madly splashed around me as I ran toward shore.

All the boys looked our way when they heard the splashing. "Hey, look at that! Two *naked* girls!" They laughed and began whistling.

One smart-ass boy came running over to the lake's rim. Realizing I wouldn't reach my things in time, I turned and went back into deeper water to conceal myself.

"Come on, girls," he teased. "I dare you to come on out of there."

I could feel the heat of embarrassment spread across my face as I turned to Lori. She stood smiling at the boy calm as could be. "Only if you walk away," she said.

The boy turned and saw our clothes by the base of a tree. He looked back at us with a sly grin on his face, "Okay, I'll walk away," then he quickly scooped up our belongings and took off running.

Lori shoved her drink at me and said, "Hold this," then ran out of the water, completely nude and chased him. I sank lower in the water, mortified. Lori caught up with the kid, hit him and got our attire back. He ran back to his friends, laughing all the way.

Lori came back, dropped my clothes at the base of the tree and quickly dressed herself. "Come on, Bonny. The coast is clear."

I looked over and saw the boy had rejoined his friends. As I moved closer to shore, they were no longer in sight. "Okay."

I emerged from the water and grabbed my things. "Thanks, Lori. Man, you have balls!"

Lori laughed as I finished dressing. "Hey, I wasn't going to let him take our clothes. No big deal. Come on."

We started walking toward the parking lot. "Well, Lor, all I can say is, you've got more nerve than I do."

Once we reached my car, I poured the remaining sloe gin into our cups and tossed the empty pint into a trash barrel before Lori and I nonchalantly walked over to join the boys.

The guys had set up a pony keg on the back bed of the truck. Those boys were so cocky. They bragged that nobody was going to catch them. Yeah, right.

Over the next few hours, they tried to one-up each other and made stupid jokes. Maybe it was the booze, but Lori and I couldn't stop laughing. As the sun started to set, we decided to head home. Lori and I had just opened the doors to my car when all of the sudden we heard, "Oh *shit*! *Cops*!" Gravel dust flew as two police cars quickly blocked the truck from making an escape.

The cops eye-balled the keg and yanked the boys off the truck, handcuffing and shoving them in the backseat of the cruisers.

Standing next to our car and clutching our near-empty drinks, Lori and I were as nervous as two deer surrounded by a pack of hungry wolves when the police noticed us. "What do you have in your cups?" one officer demanded.

Finding my voice, I answered, "Slurpees." I tipped my cup toward him so he could see the melted red slush.

"Okay. The park is closing now. Get in your car and leave."

We were happy to oblige. "Yes sir." I responded.

Lori stood frozen in place.

Between smiling, clenched teeth I said, "Lori, get in the car, *now!*"

She got in and we took off and drove until we found a church parking lot. I brought the car to a stop and shut off the engine.

Both Lori and I were still trembling. "I'm so glad you answered them," Lori's voice shook, "I wouldn't have thought of that."

"I'm just glad they didn't come too close to smell our breath or look in the trash can and find that empty pint! Between getting our clothes stolen and the near-arrest, we were very lucky tonight. We would have been in s-o-o-o much trouble! How about a cigarette to calm our nerves?"

"Yeah," Lori said, as we both lit up.

Bonny Brookes

7
DEVASTATION

With autumn came changes. Andrew moved to Utah and I moved from my first apartment to a college dorm room. We no longer kept in touch.

Once at college, I quit smoking and stopped doing all the crazy, wild things of my earlier teen years. I wanted to get through college, have a career and do something with my life I'd be proud of. At that time, however, I had no idea what career I should pursue. I hoped taking the various college courses would help me figure it out.

Without a high school diploma, Lori didn't have any luck finding a job until her father hired her to join her mother and siblings at the family's drugstore. Lori spent her days behind the cosmetic counter.

Outside of work, Lori continued partying and had no real goals or strong dreams for her life. Even though we spent time together during my freshman-year college holidays and summer break, we were heading down different roads.

CRSD

As I studied for finals on a mid-December morning of my sophomore year, the phone rang in the dorm room. I didn't move as I knew one of my roommates would grab it. "Bonny, it's for you!" I rolled off my bed to go find out who was calling.

"Hello?"

"Bon! On my God," Lori wailed, "Bon! My *Dad*!"

"Lori, take a deep breath. What's wrong? Something with your dad?"

"My *Dad*. He had a heart a—" A huge sob escaped her. She gulped in air then continued, "Heart attack. We were all working at the drugstore, and he stood at the prescription counter in the pharmacy, where he always is, and . . . ," Lori stopped. I waited patiently for her to continue. ". . . suddenly, he just crumpled to the ground, like a deflated Bozo clown. Oh *Bon*!"

"Is he at the hospital?"

"He's *dead*!" Lori screamed. "We all saw him die. Even with the hospital right across the street, it didn't matter. He died from a massive heart attack right in front of us. Bon, can you please come home?"

"Of course, Lori. I'll leave here within the hour and be there as soon as I can. I love you."

"Love you, too."

I told my professor there had been a death in the family. A white lie, yes, but Lori's family was like my family. He agreed to let me make up the final exam later. I had over an hour's drive in the wintry weather to my hometown. I traveled as fast as I dared down the ice-patched two-lane country roads surrounded by ten-foot-deep ditches; ravines some drivers ended up in. Snowflakes started falling. I continued on. I needed to be with Lori. I owed her that. She had been there for me when my mother died.

I entered the house and found Lori's mother quietly speaking with some people. She glanced up and pointed toward the bedrooms. I found Lori sitting "Indian-style" on the floor of her room. She rocked back and forth. I sat next to her, wrapped my arm around her shoulders, held her and rocked with her. Tears clouded my vision as I listened to Lori's sobs.

Lori stopped rocking, took a deep breath and lit up a cigarette. "My dad is in Heaven."

"Yes, he is," I said, "but he'll always be in your heart, Lori." We had now both gone through the loss of a parent while still in our teens.

While sitting there, her cigarette smoke engulfed me. I decided not to scold her about smoking. Not now. My eyes burned and the smoke choked me, yet it still smelt good. My resolve melted as I thought, *if you can't fight 'em, join 'em.* "Lor, can I bum a smoke?" She nodded and handed me a cigarette. With the deep inhale of that first drag, I broke out coughing. It tasted horrible, but I finished it anyway.

Her father's death made mortality real for Lori. We weren't indestructible, we would all die someday. We talked in earnest about family, about the future, about our hopes and dreams.

I bummed another cigarette, then sat in silence and smoked it. This one wasn't nearly as bad as the first.

"What's the point?" she asked.

"The point?"

"About life. I mean, my dad spent all his life working hard to provide for us and making a contribution to the city while skipping vacations with his family and missing out on the things I thought really mattered. And now, he won't ever be able to retire to enjoy what he worked so hard for. What's the point? Seems like a wasted life to me." Lori fell silent then took a drag off her cigarette.

In the silence, Lori's words sank into my brain. I agreed with her; what was the point of the rat race? "Gone with or without the music being played?"

Lori gave me a puzzled look. I continued, "Your dad worked all his life to provide for others, support his family and the community, but did he do something he loved and was passionate about? Something he had a natural gift and talent for? Did he accomplish what his lifetime was intended for?

Will he be remembered?" I stopped and lit yet another cigarette. I was hooked all over again. "Lori, I think he did. He loved being a businessman, owning the drugstore and being able to make a contribution to our town. Most Saginawians know of him, and the lucky ones knew him." After taking another drag, I continued, "I think my mom left with her music unplayed. She had so much potential for either a singing, acting or writing career, but she didn't follow her dreams. Your Dad, though, I think he did. Does that make sense?"

"Yeah, it does." Lori said softly. "God's gift to us is our unique talent. He gives it to us to use while here on Earth, yet most people never use it and some never even discover it because they are so hung up on either chasing money or doing what they think society expects them to do."

"Exactly."

"I don't want to die without my music being played."

"Me, neither."

Lori talked about her big picture. She wanted to use her creative abilities to bring joy to others. She also wanted to settle down, get married and maybe even have kids. She wanted to matter to someone, to be loved. She wanted her life and talents to make a difference to those around her. I did, too.

8
NEW BEGINNING

After completing my sophomore year of college, I returned home for summer break and to my old job at 7-11. Now that I lived back home, when I wasn't working, I spent most of my free time with Lori. Our favorite hangout, the Alibi, had closed and in its place stood a fruit stand. We soon found a new hang out, an old golf course clubhouse recently converted into an upscale bar.

Located at the edge of the Tittabawassee River, the elegant, one-story brown wooden building stood on piers with a wall of windows overlooking the water as it lazily passed under the cover of large old hardwood trees lining the banks. But we didn't notice because we only went there at night.

At this bar, we met tons of young adults from all over town, including two guys: Matt and Larry.

Matt had gone to my high school, but graduated a year before me, so I had never really gotten to know him. He had blonde hair and green eyes and I felt tall next to this little guy who stood maybe five foot three.

His friend, Larry, had gone to a different school. Lori liked Larry from the moment she met him. Larry had shoulder-length brown hair, stood a few inches taller than Lori, had a little girth around his middle and sported a two-day-old beard. He didn't talk much, nor did he smile often, which earned him the nickname "Grouch." But Lori liked him. He listened to her, letting her ramble on and on and they discovered they had a lot in common. She began spending most of her time with him.

One early afternoon, Lori stopped by my house. We sat on the back patio watching all the construction crews pushing dirt around with their bulldozers in the field soon to be filled with houses.

"Bon, I'm going out with Larry tonight," Lori began.

"There's a big surprise!" I said. "Where are you guys going?"

"We're going over to a friend of a friend's house . . . and well, it's not just us. Larry's good friend is coming to. You know, Matt."

"Matt, the guy who went to my high school?"

"Yeah."

Little Matt, I thought. Of course, standing as straight as possible, I only reached five feet, still I preferred guys at least five foot six and he wasn't. Yet, with his blond hair and green eyes, Matt was adorable. From what I remembered of him from the night at the club, he was also very nice and had a great sense of humor.

"I think you two would be so cute together."

I shook my head. "Lori!"

She persisted, "Why not? You're both short, you're both cute and you both went to the same high school. That's a start!"

I laughed at her enthusiasm. "No, Lori."

"Why not?"

"I'll tell you what, how about I meet you and Larry and Matt over at the house of Matt's friend. Would that work?"

"I guess it'll have to." Lori said as she wrote directions to the party and handed them to me. "Here. Now go figure out what you're going to wear and I'll do the same. I'll see you there at nine."

CR80

Three brothers shared the old two-story gray farmhouse out on the edge of town. One of the brothers graduated with Matt. When I arrived, Lori and Larry stood waiting for me next to his car. The place was a-rocking! Partygoers filled the house and yard, rock music blared and a line formed near the keg in the dirt driveway. I recognized a lot of faces from high school. Several of the guys brought their guitars and let me sit in with them. Soon someone turned off the stereo so our live entertainment of folksy guitar music could be heard. Although, I'd only been playing about a year, I loved being included with the group.

After I played along to the only songs I knew by memory, they declared it was time for a "band" break. With my performance done, I looked around the house for Lori. Instead, I found Matt in the large country-styled kitchen.

"Hey, Matt, have you seen Lori?"

"Yeah, she and Larry are sitting outside with some others." Matt looked directly at me, "Hey, I didn't know you played guitar."

"I'm still learning. The guys are really good though, aren't they?"

"Yeah. You wanna go outside and get a beer?"

"Sure."

Matt and I walked outside, found Lori and Larry and joined them and some other guests in the front yard. We all stayed well past midnight.

Parties occurred weekly at the farmhouse and it became our new *Alibi* that summer. But "we" now included Grouch most of the time. Even though Matt sometimes also joined us, we never got together or double-dated, despite Lori's constant attempts.

As the summer progressed, Lori spent more and more of her time with Larry. One day that summer, in early August, Lori and I walked over to "our" field. I seemed to be doing all the jabbering while Lori didn't say a word. When we reached the "Umbrella Tree," I sat down resting my back against the tree with my legs extended out in front of me, while Lori wrapped her arms around her folded legs and rested her chin on her knees. I could tell by her lack of conversation and now, by the way she was sitting, she was either worried or had something she wanted to talk about.

"Lori, what's up? You haven't said a word."

After a few minutes, Lori turned to me. "I want to tell you, but I don't know where to start."

"Start at the beginning," I said as I pulled a cigarette out of my purse.

"Well, you know Larry . . ."

"Yes, I think I know him," I teased her.

"Well, you know we're together almost twenty-four seven now . . ."

"No, I hadn't noticed." Lori's hesitance was driving me nuts. "Come on Lor, spit it out. Are you getting married?"

Lori looked down at the dirt as she drew stick figures in the dust and finally replied, "Maybe."

"Maybe? Did he ask you?" My excitement grew, but her obvious reluctance confused me.

"Not yet. But I think he will, when—" Lori looked up at me with tears in her eyes.

I didn't have a clue on what Lori wanted to share, but it didn't sound like good news now. "Lori, what is it? Is something wrong?"

"I'm pregnant."

A rush of emotions streamed through me. I didn't know whether to laugh, cry, twirl Lori around or sit quietly. I opted to remain calm.

"Okay, so you're pregnant. You'll be nearly twenty-one when you give birth. It's okay. Do you want to have the baby?"

"Yes, with every fiber of my being. But . . ." Lori went back to drawing stick figures in the dirt.

"But what?" I prodded.

"What if Larry doesn't want to have the baby? What if he won't marry me? What am I going to do?"

"Larry doesn't know about the baby?"

"No."

"Lori, you've got to tell him. He has a right to know. And you know what?" Lori looked up from the dirt but didn't say anything. "Larry just may surprise you. He may want to have this baby as much as you do. Just tell him—today."

"You think?" Lori asked as if she didn't really believe what I had said.

"I think. Let's go back to my house. You can call him from my room. Nobody's there, and I'll go outside, so you can have privacy. Sound like a plan?"

"Yeah. And, Bon, thanks for being my friend."

"Anytime."

When Lori came out into the backyard after talking with Larry, she had a huge smile on her face. "You were right. He's willing to talk and he's coming over right now to take me out to dinner so we can decide what to do."

"See, I told you! Things will work out, if you just believe they will."

Several minutes later, we heard Larry pull into the drive. "He's here," we both said at once. We quickly walked around to the front of the house. I waved hello to him and gave Lori a big squeeze, before she climbed into Larry's car and off they went.

The following morning, I called Lori to find out what happened.

"Oh, Bon, we're getting married!"

I smiled knowing Larry had come through for Lori, just as I had predicted. "That's fantastic! Congratulations."

"Hang on just a sec," Lori said. I could hear her lighting up a smoke. "Ah, Bonny . . ."

"Yeah?"

"Well, I don't want you to be hurt or mad, but . . ."

"What is it?"

"I always thought I'd have a big wedding and have you as my maid of honor . . . but . . ."

Lori's hesitancy made me wonder what was going on. "But?"

She took a deep breath then blurted out "Well, we're going to go to the JP with only two witnesses, our mothers. Please don't be mad or hurt."

I chuckled, "Oh, is that it? I'm not hurt, Lori. What matters is that you're happy. Do what's right for *you*."

"You're such a great friend. Thanks for understanding, Bon."

"No problem."

A few days later, after getting their blood tests and marriage license, Lori and Larry were married and I returned to college to begin my junior year.

9
PARTY PREMONITIONS

L ori gave birth to a beautiful, happy baby girl, Marie, while I was away at college. Though there never was a formal baptism, Larry and Lori announced that Matt was the godfather and I was the godmother. I felt honored.

Lori stopped working at her job to focus on her daughter. That baby meant the world to Lori. She fussed over her, bought her outfits and wouldn't let the baby out of her sight. Larry either worked or went off partying with his friends, so most of Lori's time she spent alone with Marie.

CR80

Three months after Marie's birth, I returned home from college for summer break. My major had been elementary education, yet after working as a teacher's aide in a second grade classroom during my last semester, I realized it wasn't for me. I needed to rethink my major and career goals, and wanted to take a year off from college to work and save money. With Father's help, I landed a great full-time job working as a customer service rep at an insurance company.

During my time in college, Father had sold our old house and moved into a large, beautiful brown-brick storybook-design home with his new wife, Angie—the former student of his, and her teen-aged children. Time had begun to mend the pain and we were all moving on.

Upon moving home though, I quickly realized I was not adapting well to living at the new house with Father's new family. My brother and I both felt like outsiders. By then, Scott had stopped blaming me for our mother's death and agreed to rent a place with me. We found a two-bedroom pink-brick duplex with white shutters, a bright sunny kitchen, a huge yard and even a garage. My brother and I signed a one-year lease and moved in.

Surprisingly, this time Father agreed to let my brother and I bring Thomasina with us. I think Father knew she'd receive more love and attention from Scott and me. Unfortunately, because of her advanced age, she had a hard time seeing and bumped into walls of the unfamiliar surroundings, couldn't find her box and had trouble jumping on the bed. So, within a few weeks, we had no choice but to return her to Father. At least at his house she knew her way around and had plenty of places to lie in the sun while hiding from the commotion and all the new faces that didn't particularly like cats. Though I missed her, it was best for Thomasina.

I was excited to be back in town and when I wasn't working, I spent most of my extra time with Lori.

附

On a Friday evening after working at the insurance company all day, I dropped by Lori's. She let me in and I saw Marie giggling and playing with toys that Lori had spread all around her on a blanket on the floor. There was no sign of Larry.

"Is Larry at work?"

"Yep."

"So how's life, Lor?"

She gave me a half-hearted smile, then led the way to the dining room table. "Okay, I guess," she said as we both sat down.

A series of giggles erupted and we both looked over at Marie. She was having a ball. "Marie's happy!" I said.

Lori watched her daughter a moment with a look of pure joy on her face. "Yeah, she's the best thing in my life."

"And that's the way it should be."

Lori lit up a cigarette then walked over to the refrigerator to grab a beer. "Do you want one? It's happy hour."

"Sure," I said while watching Marie play.

Lori sat back down, opened both beers and handed me one.

"So when does Larry usually come home?"

"It's Friday."

"Yeah . . ."

"Well, that means I don't know when he'll be home."

"Why?"

"Oh, Bon." Lori took a long sip of beer. "I try to keep a good face to the world and make everyone believe life is perfect, but it's not."

"I thought you guys were doing great. You're not?"

Lori shook her head. "He works during the week, which is great, because he is a good provider, but . . ."

"But what?"

Lori looked at Marie, who was rolling on her back with her hands and legs in the air playing with a bear with a little drum, then looked back at me. "I don't think he's cheating on me or anything, but he just prefers to go out and party with the guys on the weekend rather than be with us."

"Well—" I took a chug of beer buying time to think of something encouraging to say. "As long as he's faithful to you, Lor."

She looked at me. I could tell she knew that I didn't understand her pain. "It's just that when he is here, he expects me to wait on him hand and foot. But yet he never helps with the baby." Lori stopped and took another drink. "It's like I'm taking care of two children with nothing in return. I'm beginning to resent him for that."

"Have you told him how you feel?"

"I tried. I told him she's his daughter too and he should help."

I looked directly at Lori and asked, "And what did he say?"

"Nothing. He left. He spends the weekends out until the wee morning hours. He's never here to help and I feel like I'm a single mother."

I grasped for anything that would put a positive spin on the situation and said, "At least he pays the bills."

Lori grunted. "Yeah, but I'm still alone with Marie. I love her deeply, but yet I'm lonely. Does that make sense?"

"Yeah. Yeah, it does."

"I just wish he would be here so we could be a real family. But he's not, and I don't know what to do to make him want to come home to be here with us."

I didn't know what to say, so said nothing and only nodded.

☙❧

In late August, as usual, I stopped by Lori's after work on a Friday evening. Lori opened the door with a huge smile on her face.

"What's up with the big smile Lori? Something exciting happen today?"

"Well, no, but I've come up with a plan."

I walked toward the table and sat down. "A plan for what?"

Lori went into the kitchen, grabbed two beers then joined me. Marie, once again, was happily playing on her blanket on the living room floor. "You know how I love making a big deal out of holidays and birthdays, so they are special?"

I cracked open the beer and took a drink then nodded.

"Well, you know Marie will be six months old next month."

"Don't tell me, you want to throw a six-month-old birthday celebration."

"Well, yeah! Do you think anyone would come?"

"Maybe other mothers, family, and, of course, me."

Lori looked at Marie then took a drink. "I was thinking of something a little bit bigger than that."

"Like what?"

"Well, I figure the best way to keep Larry home is to invite his friends over here."

"That might work."

We began brainstorming on who to invite, and by the time I left, Lori had about thirty calls to make. Over the weekend she spent hours on the phone calling to invite everyone she could think of to her daughter's birthday party.

The day of the party, Lori was doing what she loved best, being creative. She designed banners and decorations and hung them all over the living room. Then she made the cake, from scratch.

Guests starting arriving. By nine, partygoers packed into the small apartment. Smoke filled the air. People puked in the bathroom. Beer cans and empty bottles littered the countertops. The stereo blared and folks yelled to be heard over the music. As midnight approached, none of the guests appeared to have the common courtesy of knowing when to leave—especially with an infant sleeping in the bedroom.

Lori grabbed my arm and said, "Let's get some fresh air and talk," and then pulled me out into the hall. Once the apartment door closed behind us, she asked, "How can I get these people to go, without coming off as a bitch?"

Lori sat down at the top of the stairwell. I sat next to her and said, "Look, you have a baby in there. The loud voices and the overwhelming smoke aren't good for her. Just tell them to take the party elsewhere . . . and if nobody listens, I'll be the bitch."

"Oh, would you really be the bitch? That'd be great. Will you?"

Before I could answer, Matt came out into the hall. "Hi Matt," we said in unison.

"Too smoky in there for you?" I asked him as he leaned against a structural pole across from us.

"Yeah, a little. Actually, I saw you two come out here and I wanted to talk to you."

"Yeah, about what?" Lori asked him.

"I've been having some really weird dreams lately," Matt began. "I haven't told anyone, but I know you two won't laugh at me and tell me I'm demented."

I searched his green eyes as I asked, "What happens in your dreams, Matt?"

"Weird stuff. Like being pulled by hands, but I can't see who is pulling me. It's just really weird. I keep getting this feeling, like . . . I'm gonna die."

"Oh, Matt," Lori said. "You're not going to die. Maybe it's something to do with your work, or pressures you're feeling."

"Maybe," Matt said as he studied the carpeting in the stairwell, "but you know I have diabetes. Maybe it has something to do with that?"

"Matt, you're only twenty-three years old. Go to the doctor if you're concerned, but I'm sure it's nothing." Lori got up and smiled at me then headed for the door. "Okay, Bon, time to go be a bitch!"

I looked at Matt and our eyes locked. He was serious and I could see his fear. Without a word, I hugged him then followed Lori into the apartment.

As promised, I kicked everyone out. Lori's husband went with the crowd, but I hung around to help Lori clean up, before I left, exhausted.

A few days after the party, Matt's words continued haunting me. I had an overwhelming urge to check on him, so I drove over to his mother's house and found him in the driveway mixing cement for a construction project. I didn't want to interrupt his work, so shortly after saying hello, I left, feeling relieved. Matt seemed fine.

Exactly two weeks after checking on Matt, I flipped on the TV and flopped on the couch to relax for a bit after a long day at work. Mew, my newly adopted twelve-week-old kitten, climbed up the side of the couch then snuggled in the crook of my arm. I stroked his little head while I watched the evening news.

A news report flashed across the screen. I watched as paramedics removed a man from a car that had crashed into a median. At first, all I could see were boots and legs, followed by a limp torso. Then, a name appeared in bold letters at the bottom of the screen. Matt?

I jerked up, knocking Mew to the carpet then froze as I stared at the TV. Chills swept down my spine. Matt was dead. "No! Oh my God, he knew!" I ran to the phone and called Lori.

She answered laughing and I could hear Marie giggling in the background.

"Lor, are you watching TV?"

"No, why? What's up?"

I took a deep breath to steady my nerves, then said, "Lor, sit down."

"Bon?"

"Matt's dead."

"No! Oh my God! How?"

"Car accident. It was on the news."

"Oh wow." Lori paused. "He knew . . ."

"Yeah."

"I'm going to call Larry. I don't know how he's going to take this."

"Lor, if you need me to babysit, let me know."

She was silent for a moment. "Ah, yeah. I'll let you know. I need to call Larry."

After Lori called her husband, she called back and asked me to meet them at the farmhouse. They had a sitter.

Thirty minutes later, Matt's other good friend stepped out of the back door as we climbed out of our cars in the driveway. Visibly shaken, he told us Matt had been there earlier acting kind of strange. He had insisted Matt eat a peanut butter and jelly sandwich, because he thought Matt's sugar might be out of whack. Matt ate it, but then got into his car and said he needed to go. He could not be stopped. Later we learned, Matt had gone into a diabetic coma and probably had already been dead when his car hit the cement divider on the highway.

We were all shaken, all crying, all hugging. Lori and I looked at each other. Nobody else knew what Matt had been thinking and so scared of . . . just a few weeks ago. "I think we should tell them," I said.

"Tell us what?" Larry asked.

Lori shared Matt's premonition. The guys looked at her dumbfounded. The outside temperature had dropped to below freezing, so we went inside to the kitchen, had a beer and then spent the next hour sharing stories of Matt—our private memorial service to him.

Just months after her birth, Marie's godfather had joined her grandfather in heaven.

10
LIFE GOES ON

Lori and I sat, as usual, at the table and watched Marie, who now walked everywhere to explore her world.

"Lor, I'm going to Florida to visit my grandparents in two weeks. They said I could bring a friend and I want you to come with me. It will be so much fun!"

"Bon, I can't."

"Why not? Think about it, Lori. Larry, or maybe your mother or one of your sisters could watch Marie, and it'd be good for you to have a break. It's only ten days out of your life."

"No, it won't work." she said as she lit up a cigarette. "I don't like traveling, and plus, didn't I tell you we're moving?"

"No!" I said while looking over at Marie who had found an interesting framed photo and plopped down on her bottom as she admired it. "Where? When?"

"We found a larger apartment in a nicer part of town."

"That's great! When are you moving?"

"About the time you'll be in Florida."

I was disappointed. I really wanted Lori to come, but now I knew she really couldn't. "Oh."

We talked a while longer, Lori gave me her new address and then she had to start packing for their move, so I left.

Two weeks later, I climbed aboard a Greyhound bus for my first big trip across the country, alone.

I spent most of my time in Florida lounging next to the pool reading magazines, though I did experience a greyhound dog race in Tampa and saw an alligator sliding into the golf course pond near my grandparent's condo.

When I boarded the Greyhound bus to return home, I had a deep, dark tan. Three days later, I arrived home wearing the clothes I left Florida in. My first goal was taking a shower to remove the dust and grime from my travels. As the cleansing water cascaded over me, I noticed most of my tanned skin going down the drain.

Once dressed, I headed over to Lori's new apartment to tell her about the trip. I immediately loved their new apartment. She had such a flair for decorating and housekeeping, the place was spotless, while being inviting and cozy.

Marie played quietly in her new playpen in the middle of the living room. "Lor, I'm back and, wow, Florida is so cool!"

"Tell me about your trip."

I told her about the bus ride, the dog race I went to, the alligator and the wonderful weather. I finally stopped, realizing I had hogged the entire conversation. I looked at her. "Lori, what's going on in your world? Why's Marie in a playpen? And—" I paused as I looked directly at her, "something about you is different."

Lori laughed as she leaned over the playpen and picked up Marie. "Well, Marie is in a playpen so she stops rearranging everything for me!" Lori settled Marie on her lap and combed her hair. Marie loved the attention. "And I look different? Well, I do I have a surprise to share with you!"

"I love surprises. What is it?"

Lori's face broke out into a big grin and with a twinkle in her eye, she whispered over Marie's head, "We're expecting!"

"Oh, Lori! I'm so happy for you. You are a wonderful mother, and this little baby will bring you so much joy! When are you due?"

"Late October."

"I'm going back to college this fall, but I'm only an hour away at school, so just call me, and I'll be here!"

"You know I will!"

CRSO

Our town had seen its ups-and-downs over the past century. At one time, it flourished as a lumber town, then as the place for manufacturing steering equipment for automobiles. But, with the advent of the computer, thousands of factory jobs were eliminated, resulting in sky-high unemployment in the area. Many of the unemployed turned to drinking and drugs to calm their anxieties. Crime and violence committed by the unemployed became common evening news fare. Eventually the harshness of the current world crept into our personal lives.

"Bon, I'm calling with sad, no . . . sick, news."

"Are you sick Lori? Is the baby okay? Marie?"

"I'm fine, Marie and the baby in my belly are fine. But, do you remember Star—you know, Jessica?"

Jessica had dated a high school friend of mine. After graduation, though, they had broken up, and Lori and I only saw Jessica now and then with some other man neither of us knew. "Well, Star bought a lottery ticket, which turned out to be a winning ticket—of a few hundred dollars." I could hear Lori take a puff off a cigarette.

"Well, that's kind of happy, not sad news, Lori," I said. "I'm guessing there's more?"

"Yeah. Her boyfriend, who's unemployed and a druggie, demanded Star split the winnings. He seemed to think the money was his. She refused. In his drug-induced state, he grabbed the samurai sword off the wall above their fireplace mantel and plunged it through her. Jessica died."

Lori had shared the news in a very detached and clinical manner. I understood why. We had both suffered huge losses in our lives and never wanted to feel that pain again. As a way of self-preservation, we tried to disconnect from our emotions. Yet, I had visualized what Lori described. "Oh my God!"

"The funeral is in three days. Do you think you can make it?"

"No, Lori, I really can't." Though I'd known Jessica, she wasn't a real close friend, and I couldn't afford missing classes to attend her funeral. "I'm sorry."

"No, don't be sorry. I thought I'd go if you went, but I don't think I'm going either."

⋘⋙

When the phone rang a few months later, I thought it was just a friendly "I miss you" call from Lori. We had gotten in the habit of talking for about twenty minutes on a weekly basis.

"Bon, I've got some news."

"News? Good news?"

"No."

"Nothing like Jessica, right?"

"No . . . yeah . . . worse."

"Worse? How can anything be worse than being murdered at the hands of your boyfriend?"

"Well, this one was also murdered at the hands of her boyfriend, but this time it's a closer friend." I could hear Marie crying in the background. "Hang on a minute." Marie stopped crying and Lori returned to the line. "Bon?"

"Yeah, I'm here."

"Anyway, you remember Sue, right?"

Sue had been in my brother's class, but both Lori and I had become good friends with her after she graduated from high school. Sue was very sweet and always had a smile on her face.

"Yes. Sue's dead?"

"Yes, but Bon, how she died makes my stomach churn."

"I don't know if I want to hear this . . . but go ahead."

"Her boyfriend was extremely jealous. He thought Sue was cheating on him—she wasn't—but he didn't believe her. From what I understand, he came home stoned out of his mind, grabbed some scissors, started accusing her of seeing someone else and then began stabbing her." Lori paused. "It gets worse."

"How can it get worse?"

"When the police arrived, they found blood trails leading from the living room where her boyfriend had first started stabbing her to the bathroom where she had barricaded herself from him. They found Sue's bloody hand prints sliding down the back of the bathroom door, and then parts of Sue, in bits and pieces, scattered around the bathroom lying in pools of blood."

As I listened, what played in my mind made me want to throw up. "Lor, I'm gonna puke. Hang on a sec." I swallowed hard several times to prevent myself from regurgitating. "Lor, that makes me sick, literally."

"Yeah, me too. The jerk that did this to her actually called the cops and said something like, 'I think she's dead. I don't know, nothing is wiggling.' When the cops arrived, they got sick too. I heard they had to step outside and throw up after discovering her remains. Her poor mother is really grieving. At least that bastard is locked up and hopefully, he'll spend his life behind bars, or better yet, somebody shoots his rotten ass. He doesn't deserve to live after what he did to such a sweet person."

A moment of silence passed as we both became lost in our thoughts. "Is there going to be a memorial service?" I asked.

"I don't know yet. I'll let you know."

"Okay. Hopefully I can make it."

I could see Sue's smiling face in my mind, yet seeing her as Lori had described was too much. I needed to get ready to go to work, a part-time job as a birthday hostess at McDonald's I'd taken to cover my living expenses while attending school, so I had to stop all thoughts of what Lori had shared, for now.

It turned out I was unable to go to Sue's funeral because of class and work conflicts. Lori went without me.

ভপ্তভ

I came home the first weekend in October to visit with Lori since her due date was getting close. I went home first and within minutes of walking in the house, I noticed Thomasina didn't come to greet me.

I called out to my father who was working in his basement office.

"Is that you, Bonny?"

"Yeah, Dad I'm home." I heard my father coming up the stairs. When he got to the top of them, I asked, "Where's Tommy?"

He avoided my eyes and simply said, "She's gone."

"What do you mean *gone?*"

"Well, she got outside and we didn't notice, and she's been gone for weeks now. I figured because she was so old, she probably ran away to die."

I was furious at my father for not telling me immediately, but didn't say a word. Instead, I ran upstairs and quickly created flyers and then went door-to-door asking neighbors if they'd seen her. I hung posters and called to her until the sun started to set, with no luck. My hope had begun to fade of finding her. I went back to the house and called Lori.

"Lor?"

"Bon? What's wrong? You sound like you're going to cry."

My last hope of finding the cat suddenly died and the tears flowed. Lori waited and then said, "Bonny. Tell me what's wrong."

I sniffed loudly then said, "It's Thomasina. She's gone."

"Gone? Is she lost?" Lori knew how much I loved animals, especially the cat I'd had since I was seven years old.

"Dad said she got out. I've been all over the neighborhood. Nobody's seen her." I took a deep breath. "I think she's dead, Lori."

"Oh, Bon. I'm so sorry."

"Thanks. I know it must sound weird, but besides my dad and brother, Tommy was the only consistent part of my life. Unlike them though, she loved me unconditionally."

"Animals are special in that way."

"Yeah." I took a breath and looked out the window to see the night sky. "Lor, I'm really sorry, but I don't think I'll be able to visit you. Next time, okay?"

"You got it."

I returned to school the next day and cried on and off over the next few days as I came to accept my cat's death. Another part of my heart had been ripped away and only when I visualized Thomasina held in my mother's arms in heaven, did it make the pain bearable.

That next weekend I met a very attractive guy with shoulder-length dark hair, green eyes and a square jawline. He stood about ten inches taller than I and was a member of the "brother" fraternity to my sorority. I was a year older than Dave, but it didn't matter. We both loved to roller-skate and started roller "dancing" weekly. We'd sway to the music, and then start the acrobats. He'd pull me through his legs, lift me, or we'd spin or quickly maneuver direction from forward to backward to forward again, always keeping together. It was such fun. The more time we spent together, the more we discovered how many other things we had in common.

Six weeks after we'd met, a car accident killed Dave. Losing a parent and a pet, although hard, is somewhat expected. Not expected are the deaths of friends. The deaths of Matt, Star, Sue, and now, my new boyfriend in such a short span of time left me feeling apprehensive about the future. I couldn't help but wonder who would be next.

I wanted to escape Michigan's depressing gray skies, its bitter cold air and the constant deaths. I needed sunshine, warm weather and a fresh start. Many others seemed to agree with me. A sticker had recently begun appearing on car bumpers that read *The last one to leave Michigan, please turn out the lights*. I agreed wholeheartedly. I needed to tell Lori my plans, but first I needed to figure them out.

CRR80

A week later Lori called to announce the birth of her new son, Ken. Finally, some good news, and boy, did I need it.

"I think he looks like me."

"Yeah? Brown eyes? Blond hair?"

"Well," Lori laughed, "His eyes are blue right now and his hair is dark, but those things change. I was talking more about his nose and chin and face in general."

"Oh. Okay. I don't know when I can make it back home, Lor, but I'd love to see him. Would you mail me a picture?"

"Sure, I just don't know when it will be. With two kids now, time is limited . . . but I'll try." Lori paused before adding, "I wondered if you would be his godmother?"

"Of course, Lori! I'm honored."

"Good. I wasn't sure, since we don't get together very much anymore."

My heart filled with happiness for her. She had what she wanted: a husband and two kids. Me, on the other hand, that was the last thing on my mind. I wanted to get out of Michigan, get a fresh start, and maybe, just maybe, sometime after graduating from college, meet someone and settle down. That was a long way off though.

It wasn't until Christmas break I finally had the time to visit Lori and meet her little son. When I cradled Ken in my arms for the first time, he was already two months old.

"He *does* look like you, Lori!"

With a touch of pride in her voice, she said, "I thought so."

"Lor, I have some news."

"Yeah?" Lori said as she reached her finger out for Ken to wrap his pudgy baby hand around.

I told her about my intention of taking a break from college and heading south to Austin, Texas.

"Why?" she asked.

"I don't like it here. The days are gray, the air is cold and people are leaving by car or coffin. I need a break."

Lori removed her finger from Ken's grasp and went to peek in on Marie napping on the bed, then returned and stood next to the sofa looking down at her son in my arms. "Where will you live? What will you do?"

"I'll figure it out when I get there. I'm not too worried. It's only for a semester, Lor, I'll be back."

"You'd better . . . who would I have to talk to?"

"There's this little thing called a telephone . . ."

"Yeah, yeah."

Bonny Brookes

11
DREAMS & DISAPPOINTMENTS

I arrived in Austin, Texas, on New Year's Eve. It was seventy degrees out and I loved it instantly! The first two nights, I stayed with some friends then quickly found an efficiency apartment near the University of Texas. That same day, a criminal attorney hired me to be his secretary/ bookkeeper. I'd taken a leap of faith quitting school and moving here and had landed on my feet.

"Hey, Lor, I'm here!"

"What's it like?"

"Well, you know that commercial with the two eggs?"

"The ad showing one egg in its shell representing a brain, and the other egg frying in a pan that's meant to be a brain on drugs, and then they say 'any questions?'"

"That's the one. So, the egg frying represents hell, that would be Saginaw; and the other egg represents paradise, that would be Austin. Any questions?"

"So, I take it you like Austin."

"I love it! I'm wearing shorts today, Lori, and it's the middle of *winter*!"

❀

During my time in Texas, I discovered calling long distance wasn't cheap. A new long distance service had come out that drastically reduced the cost of long distance calls, but not everyone had that service. Lori didn't. I phoned her as often as I could, at least once a month, sometimes, a lot more to get updates on the kids and her life.

Lori was homebound with two small children and got lonely. Being so far away, I didn't think there was anything I could do to help, except listen.

And, I listened . . . a lot, and for several hours sometimes. She told me over and over how she envied me being able to just pick up and go follow my dreams and land like a cat. I told her I felt jealous of her and her babies, and wondered if I'd ever meet a man and start a family.

"Well, the honeymoon is over," Lori shared on one of our calls.

"Why?"

"Well, Larry seems to prefer going out with the guys rather than spending time with me and our kids."

"Oh, Lor, I'm sorry, but hasn't he done that since day one? Have you talked to Larry about your feelings?" I asked.

"I tried. But then he makes me feel guilty, because he works so hard, so I can stay home with the kids, and all he is asking for is a little time for himself."

"Guilty? Okay, I do understand about wanting a little time to yourself, don't we all? But I would think he'd want to spend time with you, too. But, then again, Lori, what do I know? I'm the loser in the love department."

I could see Larry's point, but I could also see Lori's. She never had down time because she spent all her time with the kids. She wanted to spend some time with just her husband. I didn't blame her. "Lor, I really don't know what to say, except

I love you, and I'm always at the other end of the phone for you."

"Thanks, Bon. Love you, too."

CRSO

As I promised Lori, I returned to Michigan in August to finish my last year of college, but I didn't even have time to stop by to visit her before heading to my first class. Hectic described my life. I lived in an off-campus mobile home, worked three jobs to pay my bills, and carried eighteen credit hours to ensure I graduated the following spring. Unfortunately, that didn't leave much time to call Lori, let alone travel an hour to go visit her.

Four months later, over Christmas break, I finally held her son in my arms again—he was already over a year old.

"He looks even more like you now, Lori!"

"I'm glad," she said.

I detected a touch of anger in her voice and looked up from Ken to her eyes. "What's going on?"

Silence.

"Lori, something's going on. I know you too well. Please tell me. It might make you feel better," I said.

"I doubt it."

"Lor?"

"Oh, Okay."

She told me about her life, how miserable she felt because her husband was not there for her or the kids. He spent his time working or partying. And his partying now involved hard drugs. He had become a coke addict. Larry spent all the money he made on drugs, leaving nothing for the kids or Lori to live on.

"I'm at my wit's end. I don't know what to do. I don't even want him around, really. Not with his drug habit. What if he becomes violent? But on the other hand, I haven't worked in so long and my mom sold the drug store long ago. I don't know if I could even find a job, and then who would take care of my kids?" Lori rambled on. "I'm scared to death. I want to divorce him, but I'm stuck."

Lori broke down in tears. I placed Ken in the crib, checked on Marie napping in the bedroom, then sat back down next to her on the sofa and stroked her hair as she sobbed.

"Lori, I'm sure you are not meant to be miserable. There's got to be a way out of this situation. How about we brainstorm on some ways to make things better?"

"I've tried, there's no way out."

"Lor, there's always hope. And, two heads are better than one."

Lori looked at me, wiping off her tears. "I guess. Wanna beer?"

"Sure, that always helps to open up the creative juices!" I said with a smile.

Lori went into the kitchen and came back with two beers. For the next several hours, we came up with several scenarios of how she could make changes. Ultimately, she decided she needed to divorce Larry. Though I wanted to, I couldn't help her much since I lived an hour away at college. She decided to ask her mother for help. If her mother would babysit, then Lori could find a job to support herself and the kids.

Eventually, Lori did get the divorce. Unfortunately, because she had dropped out of high school just months before her graduation, she didn't have a diploma and couldn't find a job and soon found herself living in a decaying old rental house in an area of town that was iffy at best. She now collected welfare—something so foreign from how we had both been raised. She felt humiliated.

Over the next few years, Lori moved the kids from one rental to the next. Still no job. Still on welfare and food stamps.

ᘓᘓ

During my last semester in college, I visited Lori at least once a month. When we got together, we always had some beer. Yet, we also talked about very deep subjects and constantly dreamed about the future.

My college graduation quickly approached. I really wanted Lori to be there, and she told me she would come. But when the day came, she didn't. Probably because she couldn't find a sitter or afford the gas. I didn't know. Her broken promise hurt my feelings. But more important, I worried about her. What had prevented her from coming? Was she okay? I didn't know and she didn't answer my calls.

The night of my graduation, I loaded all my belongings that would fit into my car. Early the next morning I drove off, heading south to begin the next chapter of my life in Texas. Two days later, I secured a position as a claims secretary at a government contracting company and rented a cute, sun-filled one bedroom apartment just a few blocks away from the office.

As soon as I had settled in, I tried calling Lori and finally reached her. I gave her my new address and then asked her why she missed my graduation. She remained silent.

"What's going on with you, Lori?"

"I hate my life. I didn't want to burden you," Lori slurred. Evidently, she'd been drinking.

I sat with my hand on the receiver for several minutes after we hung up. I felt guilty for not being there for her. She needed someone who knew her and loved her and I was fifteen hundred miles away. I wanted to help, but didn't know how, except to call her regularly.

Lori tended to call me late at night after she'd been drinking. She hated being on welfare, hated the ratty apartments she had no choice but to live in with her kids, and began drinking more and more and more. She became a binge drinker.

One night she called and it was obvious she was two sheets to the wind. I grew very concerned, not only about her, but for her children as well. So much so, that I worked several hours of overtime during the next month in exchange for some time off in September. Then I drove the three-thousand-mile roundtrip to check on Lori and visit my father, who I hadn't spoken to recently. He was busy with work and his new family.

When I got to town, I went to Lori's place first. She now lived in an upstairs apartment behind a bar. *Great place to raise kids.* I knocked. No answer. Returning to my car, I turned on the engine and cranked up the heater. Coming from the hundred-degree heat of Texas, the fifty-degree air of Michigan caused me to shiver. I sat there in my car and waited and waited and waited.

Lori eventually came home, alone. Seeing me surprised her. She hadn't known I'd be there.

"Where are the kids?" I asked.

"At my mom's for the night."

"Oh . . . well, great, that gives us a chance to talk. I'm worried about you, Lori."

She looked away to avoid my eyes. "Don't be, I'm fine."

I knew she was lying.

"Well, come on in. Want a beer?"

"Sure. I've been on the road a long time, a beer sounds good."

We spent a few minutes on small talk. I told her about my job and described Austin. Lori didn't say much. Finally, I asked, "Why are you drinking so much these days?"

She lied, "I'm not."

"Lori, you are. Almost every time we've talked since I moved back to Texas, you've been drunk on your ass. What's going on?"

Lori held her beer can up, took a swig then looked down at the thread-bare olive-green carpeting. A few moments passed before she looked up and our eyes locked. I could see fear in her eyes. *What was she afraid of?* I wondered.

"I drink to numb the pain." Lori said at last.

"What pain? Are you sick?"

"No. Pain of being a loser. I can't find a job. I have no money. Larry is not paying child support. I just can't deal with all of this. I just can't." She broke down in tears.

"Lori, you know God doesn't give us anymore than we can handle. I know you know that."

She continued crying.

"There's a reason you're going through this, though right now you may not know why. If this doesn't kill you, you know it's going to make you stronger, right?"

Lori smiled through her tears. "Yeah."

"Okay, then. Let's come up with a plan. What kind of work have you been applying for? What kind of work do you want to do? Is going back to school an option?"

We sat up all night considering different options. Hope started to grow within her. I left an hour after sunrise and headed over to my father's house.

I stayed in town for a week and checked in on Lori frequently, giving her encouragement. I believed she wanted to stop the drinking and focus on making improvements.

Before heading back to Austin, I stopped at Lori's one last time. She opened the door, obviously drunk. I saw Ken sitting on the floor wearing diapers that desperately needed changing and heard Marie crying in another room.

Lori left the door open as she walked away to move some clothes off the couch to make a place for me to sit. I remained in the doorway, stunned. In the kitchen area, I saw dirty dishes filled the sink, in the living room laundry had been haphazardly thrown over the furniture and mail and magazines covered the dining table.

"What in the *hell* happened here?" I said as I walked in, closing the door behind me.

"I haven't had time to clean."

"What have you been doing?"

"Having a beer."

I moved closer to Lori. "Yeah, I see that. My God, you have two children here who *need* you, need you sober, and here you go and get drunk and they can be damned? You are an inconsiderate bitch!"

Marie, still crying, had wandered out into the living room. She stood at my feet and reached up to me. I picked her up, wiped off her runny nose with a tissue and then rocked her gently. Marie stopped crying and wrapped her little arms around my neck. Lori watched, but didn't say a word. "I'm going to take care of Marie then I'll be back. You should change your son's diapers." I walked into the kitchen, got Marie some juice and then carried her into the bedroom.

I set her down on the unmade bed and looked around the room. Toys and clothing covered the floor. "Marie, honey, why were you crying?"

She looked up at me as I sat next to her on the bed. "I wanted juice."

"Then everything is okay now?"

Marie smiled and nodded before she took a drink from her sippy cup.

I smiled back at her and stroked her soft, long hair as I looked around the room. I spotted a coloring book and some crayons on the floor and reached down to get them. "Marie, will you do me a favor?" She looked up at me with her big, innocent blue eyes. "Would you color a picture for me?"

"Yes!" Marie said as she grabbed the book and crayons out of my hands and flipped onto her stomach to begin her artwork.

I stood up and walked to the bedroom door. "I need to talk with your mommy for awhile."

Marie nodded but kept her eyes on the picture she had already begun to color. I closed the door behind me then headed back to Lori.

As I entered the living room, I saw Lori taking a swig from a fresh beer. I yanked the can from her hand. "Lori, you have a drinking problem. If you don't do something about it, you are going to lose your kids. Is that what you want?"

"No, but drinking makes me feel better."

"Well, all it's doing is numbing your pain for awhile. Your kids need you." Although I didn't know if what I was about to say was accurate, I thought scaring Lori might help motivate her. "If you are not willing to get the help you need, as their godmother, and for the kids' sake, I will take them both to

Texas with me, and raise Marie and Ken as my own until you get your act together."

I slammed Lori's beer can down on the coffee table and began putting diapers in the diaper bag and gathering up toys.

Lori stumbled up off the couch. "You *can't!*"

I looked her in the eyes then pointedly looked at the beer can on the table, and then back into her eyes. "Watch me."

"Okay, *okay,*" she said. "I'll get help. I swear."

I reached for the phone and handed it to her. "First call your mom to come get the kids, then call AA, get your ass off the booze, then start studying for your GED, and then maybe someone will offer you a job."

I loved Lori and wanted what was best for her. But she had to want it too. "Are you willing to do that for yourself and your precious babies?"

She nodded, took a deep breath and called her mother. She had taken the first step. Relief flowed through me.

"Lori, I've got to get on the road," I said, after her mother arrived, "but I'm calling you when I get back to Texas. I love you, and you better have done what we talked about . . . it's for the best. Okay?"

"Thanks, Bon, I do love you, and, yeah, I know it's for the best. I'll talk to you in a few days."

We hugged and I got into my car, holding the picture Marie had colored for me, and began my two-day drive back to the Southwest. I prayed Lori had the courage and willpower to do what she needed to do—for her sake, as well as for her children.

Bonny Brookes

12
BEST MISTAKE

Over the next two years, I visited Lori and my father every six months, since neither of them would visit me. I noticed when I visited Lori, her daughter played "mommy" to her little brother, and she "cleaned" house, as best as a three-year-old could. It was cute, but Marie was being more the mother than Lori. It's as if they had switched roles. Lori was blessed to have Marie in her life. She truly needed her. I felt rather sorry for Marie though, working instead of playing childhood games.

Lori coped better as time went on, but she continued going out to bars to meet and spend time around other adults. She spun extravagant stories hoping the men she met would be impressed and like her. She was terribly lonely.

Lori made a big celebration of Ken's second birthday. She'd put a lot of energy into planning the perfect party. Afterward, she had a sitter come over to watch the kids, so she could have some down time. She went to the Fordney Hotel, hoping she'd run into friends who would buy her a drink or two.

The Fordney, Saginaw's oldest building, sat on the site of the original Saginaw Fort. At one time, it had been an elegant four-story hotel that provided one of the town's only upscale bars. Now the guestrooms let as apartments to low-income renters. The bar was a dive. That didn't seem to matter to the twenty-something crowd who swarmed in nightly.

Lori walked in, wearing blue jeans and a belted sweater coat over a red and white checkered shirt, which enhanced the color of her cheeks. She had recently frizzed out her hair, as was the style, and wore her new large, brown-rimmed glasses.

She looked around the dimly lit room. A dance floor, filled with gyrating bodies, filled the center of the place, and to the side stood a few small round tables and chairs. The bar, constructed of dark polished wood, dominated the room. Several stools, bolted to the floor, ran the length of it. Behind the bar, a large mirror spanning from the ceiling down to the bar's back counter, reflected everything, giving the illusion of a much larger place. Glass shelves, in front of the mirror, supported dozens of liquor bottles.

A man with thick, shoulder-length light-brown hair and a handsome Greek nose, sat on one of the barstools. He wore a light-blue cotton shirt and blue jeans. Lori recognized him as a friend she'd not seen in years. She sneaked up behind him and then leapt into his lap. As she turned around to face him, she realized she had plopped onto a stranger's lap!

"Oops! I'm sorry. I thought you were a friend of mine." She quickly scampered off the man's lap and planted herself on the stool next to him. "Hi, I'm Lori," she said, extending her hand.

"Hi," the man smiled, "I'm Steve." They shook hands and talked for several minutes. Steve shared he worked in construction and had recently divorced.

"We're on friendly terms, though," he said while signaling to the bartender to bring them a round of drinks. "We have two elementary-aged children and share custody."

"Why did you divorce if you still like her?"

"She's a good person and good mother, but we weren't good for each other. Before we ended up hating each other and doing things that hurt both the kids and us, we got divorced." Steve took a drink. "And what's your story, Lori? I hope you're single?"

Lori took a sip of her drink before she answered. "Yes, and like you, divorced with two small children."

"How old are your children?"

"Today is my son's second birthday. I threw him a party this afternoon and he loved it . . . I think." Lori smiled. "My daughter is three. I got a sitter after the party, so I could get out and be around some grown-ups for awhile."

Steve chuckled. "I can understand that." Something about Lori appealed to him. He found he couldn't keep his eyes off of her. Rather than just stare, he asked, "and how are things between you and your ex?"

Lori looked away from Steve as she took another drink then shook her head. "Not like yours. Mine left town, he doesn't see the kids and he doesn't pay child support."

Steve searched Lori's eyes while reaching for her hand. "I'm sorry."

Lori brushed his pity off. "It's okay."

"Tell me more about you. Do you work?"

Lori, who had lots of practice spinning stories under the "Umbrella Tree" with me, gave Steve a whopper. "Well," she said, "I'm a model for Calvin Klein."

With the combination of Lori's long blond hair, brown eyes and thin physique, he didn't doubt her story. "Wow, I'm honored! Imagine, a model giving me the time of day!"

Lori smiled, pleased that he fell for her story and that he seemed interested. Over the next few hours, they talked endlessly ignoring everyone else in the bar. Steve was the perfect gentleman.

"Well, I hate to say it, Lori, but I've got to get going. Work tomorrow." He looked at Lori who was tipsy by now. "Do you have a ride home?"

"I was just going to walk. It's only a few blocks away."

"At night? I can't let my model friend run the risk of being mugged or worse, let me drive you home."

Lori agreed and soon they walked into her apartment. After paying the sitter, Lori turned on the hall light and led Steve back to the bedrooms. She cracked open a door and in a hushed voice said, "This is Ken." Steve peeked in.

In a tot bed, Ken was curled up and fast asleep. Lori quietly closed the door. Across the hall, was Lori's bedroom that she shared with her daughter. "This is Marie," she whispered from the doorway as they peered into the dark room.

"Hi Mommy!"

Lori flicked on the dresser lamp near the door. "Oh, you're awake!" she said as she walked in to give her daughter a hug. Steve followed.

Marie jumped up on her bed to hug her mother. Lori squeezed her and then said, "This is my friend. His name is Steve."

Steve moved closer to the bed and Marie looked up at him. "Hi."

"Hi."

"Mommy," Marie said turning to her mother, "Are you going to tell me a story now?"

Lori looked at her daughter, then Steve, then back to Marie. "How about if both Steve and I tell you a story?"

"Yippee!" Marie flopped down on the bed and pulled up her covers in preparation for a good, long story.

Both Steve and Lori laughed then sat on the edge of her bed.

When the story ended, which Lori and Steve had made up as it went along, Marie was still not tired. She asked Steve questions and talked to him nonstop. Before long she had wormed her way into his heart.

Lori stood up. "Honey, it's late and Steve has to go home. It's time to say good-night."

Marie's face showed her disappointment. "Already?"

"Yes."

"Okay. Bye, Steve," Marie said as she rolled over onto her side and closed her eyes.

"Bye, Marie. I enjoyed meeting you."

Lori kissed her daughter, turned out the light and then she and Steve left the room, closing the door behind them.

Steve looked at Lori as he reached for both of her hands. "Your daughter is precious. I bet she takes after her mom."

It had been so long since Lori had received a compliment, she felt herself blush.

"I really need to go, but would like to see you again."

"Okay." Lori walked over to the kitchen counter and wrote her phone number down on a scrap of paper then handed it to him. "Call me sometime."

Steve kissed Lori softly on the lips and then quietly walked out.

When he got to his truck, he found the belt to her sweater jacket. Rather than take it to her now, he held onto it—it gave him an excuse to call her tomorrow, rather than waiting the standard few days.

CRISCO

The next morning Lori called and told me in detail about meeting Steve. "He makes me feel so alive!"

"I'm thrilled for you, Lori. It sounds like you had a fantastic time . . . and he sounds like he's really a nice guy."

"He is."

"There's only one thing, Lor."

"What's that?"

"You'd better fess up about the modeling thing. I can't believe you said that!"

Lori and I both laughed. "That was good, wasn't it?"

"Yeah, and you're lucky he fell for it, but you'd better tell him the truth before you get closer. Otherwise, it could ruin everything."

"You're right. I will."

CRWSO

"So did you tell him and what'd he say?" I asked Lori several months later. I'd had trouble getting a hold of her. She seemed to never to be home. I didn't know if this was a good or bad thing.

"Hi, Bonny! Hang on a minute, hon," Lori said. I heard her set the phone down, then a moment later she was back. "I figured it's time for one of our long talks, so I got my cigarettes and I'm ready!"

"Wow, you sound in a good mood. So what happened with Steve? Did you tell him?"

"Tell him? Tell him what?"

"The modeling story."

Lori laughed. "Oh that. Yeah, I told him and we both had a good laugh over it."

"So, I take it you're still seeing him?"

"Yep." I heard Lori take a drag off her cigarette.

Suddenly I wanted one too, so I grabbed my pack, stepped outside, and lit up my smoke. "And?"

"He's the best thing ever, Bon. We have so much fun together. He doesn't really drink, so I'm not drinking near as much as I did."

"That's great, Lor!"

"Yeah, though, I'm still smoking."

"Yeah, me too."

"So, what do you two like to do together?"

"Well, it's not just the two of us normally, it's the four of us, and when Steve's kids join us, it's the six of us!"

"I bet that keeps you busy."

"It really doesn't matter what we're doing, it's just being with them. I feel needed, wanted and loved. It's a wonderful feeling, Bon."

I was happy for Lori, but I really didn't understand what she was experiencing. I found myself a little bit jealous and hoped one day I'd find what she had miraculously found by landing in the lap of a stranger.

CREED

I met several single men through my job at the construction company. One of them towered over me by almost a foot. He was good looking with dark hair and big round dark-brown eyes, but it was Ed's smile and sense of humor that won me over. He didn't come into the office often because he worked out in the field, but we spent the weekends together, along with his best friend and his girlfriend. We spent our time water-skiing or floating on rafts at the lake, or I'd fill in as Ed's caddy while he golfed or we just hung around his house, barbequed, watched golf or football, and drank beer. I didn't particularly like golf or football, but it was the only excuse I could find to be around Ed.

Despite my efforts, the relationship never grew deeper. Ed never took me out on a real date and he even told me not to come around so much. Soon after that, I discovered he had begun dating someone else. I was crushed. I thought I had been more to him than a buddy. I felt like I'd wasted two years of my life for a guy who was just stringing me along.

Due to a lack of projects, Ed was laid off and decided to return home to the state of Washington. Even though he had treated me more like a buddy than a girlfriend, once he left, I grew depressed.

A few weeks later, the company I'd worked at since my college graduation, closed its doors and I was also out of a job.

When the phone rang a week later, I expected it to be a potential job interview. "Hello?"

"Hey . . ."

"Ed?"

"Yeah. How are you?"

I was so excited to hear his voice and that he had actually called, I forgot all the reasons I shouldn't speak to him. "Hi. How am I? Well, the company shut down. So like you, I'm looking for work now." I stepped outside to my back patio to enjoy the cool breezes under the shade of trees. "Did you get a job back home?"

"No, not yet." Ed paused. The silence was uncomfortable. Finally he spoke. "Hey, I was wondering, would you have any interest in moving to Monterey?"

"Monterrey? Mexico?"

He laughed. "No, silly, the one in California. Have you ever been there?"

"No, I've never heard of it."

"Well, Pebble Beach is there, one of the best golf courses in the world, and . . ."

"And what?" I had no idea what he wanted. I didn't golf and didn't want to learn. The sport bored me.

"I'm thinking about moving there."

"Do you have a potential job there?"

"Not yet. But I really just want to play golf, so I'd take anything once I got there."

"Okay, and you're telling me this why?"

Another long, uncomfortable silence ensued before Ed spoke up. "I wondered if you'd move there and we could get back together. I don't like living at my parent's home."

"You want me to move across the country so you don't have to live with your parents?"

Ed chuckled. "Well, when you put it like that, that's not what I mean. I miss you."

His words melted my defenses. Maybe I should look into it. Look for jobs. Find out about Monterey. I really had nothing to lose. "Ed, I miss you, too. But I'm not going to move across the country without a job and a place to live. And I'm certainly not going to live with you . . . unless we're married."

"Do you want to get married?"

I didn't know if he was serious or not. My insides screamed *yes, marry him!* but my head said *he's treated you like crap, tell him to take a flying leap.* "Ed, let me think about it. Let me think about everything, okay?"

"Okay. I really do miss you. It'd be fun in Monterey. You'll see. Think about it and I'll call you in a few days."

CRSO

As always, I called Lori for her advice. "Hey, Lor. How are you doing?"

"Hi, Bon! How's Texas?"

"Well, Lor, that's why I'm calling."

"Hang on just a sec, let me turn down the TV." I lit up a cigarette while I waited for Lori. "Okay, I'm here. What's going on?"

"Well, this is going to sound crazy, but here goes." I took a deep breath. "I lost my job, the company shut down, that guy I told you about that I worked with, well he moved back to the West Coast, and now he wants me to move to Monterey, California, and even mentioned the 'm' word."

"Wow. Okay, I just felt like I was hit with repeated bullets. A lot going on in your world." I could hear Lori light up a smoke. "As far as the job, sorry to hear about that. As far as the guy, what's his name?"

"Ed," I answered.

"Okay, Ed, well do you love him?"

"I'm pretty sure I do, otherwise I wouldn't have put up with all his crap these past two years."

"Okay, well even if that is a *yes,* does he love you?"

My spirits sank. "I don't know."

"Bon, I know you too well. You're a deeply passionate person and you operate on emotions. You're going to do whatever you want to do no matter what others tell you, so what I'm going to say is based on that. *Follow your heart.* If you want to go, go; if you don't, don't. What's the worse thing that could happen?"

"I could get out there, not find a job or place to live or Ed bails on me."

"And could you live with that?"

"I would have to if it happened."

Lori knew me well. It wasn't the wisest reason to relocate, but after landing a position as a division manager at a publishing house that produced three monthly business magazines, I made the move trusting Ed would keep his promise to be there with me.

CR80

I loved my new role of managing a dozen employees and ensuring smooth operations between departments. I rented a beautiful, old white adobe tutor-styled house with a tiled roof, dark wood floors and old-fashioned roll-out windows with a view of the Pacific Ocean off in the distance. A lush green garden with orange and lemon trees filled the backyard. On the weekends, if I wasn't at Cannery Row watching sea lions and otters play in the water, I'd be in the back yard sun tanning and squeezing lemon juice into my hair every thirty minutes to bring out the gold highlights.

Ed called every weekend. We'd talk for hours and hours about our feelings and dreams. But, when I asked him specifically when he was coming, he never had a definite answer. I grew frustrated, but kept myself busy as I waited for Ed to come to Monterey.

CR80

"Bon, Steve asked me to marry him. I don't know what to do." Lori said on one of our many phone calls.

"What do you mean you don't know what to do? Do you love him?"

"Well, the kids love him, he's great with them. I love him too, but I don't know if I'm *in* love with him."

"Lor, the *in love* stuff typically fades within the first year or so. Do you like him? Do you like talking to him? Are you friends?"

"Yeah."

"Well, in the end, that's what matters most: communication, respect and friendship," I said. "But, on the other hand, what in the heck do I know, I've never been married and at this rate, probably won't ever."

Lori snickered. "Yes you will. You just haven't met him yet. Wait a minute, you moved out there for some guy, aren't you together?"

"Oh, him. Well, you see he always has a million and one reasons why he can't move here yet. And his phone calls are becoming more infrequent. At least I have a great job and a beautiful home."

"I'm sorry, Bon."

"Don't be. There's a lesson in here somewhere. Right now the two lessons I'm learning are, one, most good guys are either married, gay or dead—"

Lori burst out in laughter. "God, Bonny, you're funny!"

"No, Lori, I'm serious! And the second lesson is a guy will tell you anything to get what he wants. Steve isn't either of those, is he?"

"No."

"So, you see, Lor, you've found a good guy, you need to hang on to him!"

"So, you really think I should marry Steve?"

"Follow your heart, Lor."

"Thanks. What's that mean? My heart is all confused."

"So's mine, so don't ask me. Ask yourself, you'll figure it out."

CRQSD

On the fourth of March, Lori called to tell me she and Steve had gone to the courthouse the day before and gotten married by the Justice of the Peace.

"I'm sorry I didn't call you sooner, Bon, but we did it kind of spur of the moment," Lori explained. "We only brought our witnesses. It was real small."

"Well, it's about time, Lor! And, don't worry about not letting me know, I couldn't have gotten the time off from work anyway," I said. Although I was a little hurt, I didn't want Lori to feel guilty. "I'm just glad you finally did it! Marie and Ken love him, they need a dad and Steve is a good guy and he brings out the best in you. You did good, kid," I said smiling into the phone.

"Thanks, Bon."

"You know, I'm jealous of *you* now. You have a man and kids . . . a whole family. Me, I got nothin'."

"What about Mr. Ed?"

I laughed as I pictured the talking horse in my mind, rather than the man she referred to. "He still hasn't come to visit me! He did say he'd be down in about six weeks. So, we'll see."

"Your turn will come, I promise," Lori said.

"From your lips to God's ears!"

Lori had endured so much. She truly deserved all the happiness she now had. I was happy for her.

13
FUTURE PLANS

I flew to Saginaw to attend my ten-year high school reunion the summer of 1986. I only had forty-eight hours in town and wanted to visit Lori while there. I still had not met Steve and looked forward to finally putting a face with a name.

Lori knew I was coming, but she hadn't seen me since I moved to California. Sporting the typical Californian golden-brown tan and bleached-blond hair from the sun, salt water and lemon juice, I wondered what she'd think about my metamorphosis from a little mousy-brown brunette into a self-confident businesswoman.

I knocked on the door of Lori and Steve's apartment. Lori opened the door and looked at me for a moment before recognition set in. "Bon! Oh my God! You look great! Come on in," she said as she stepped aside and opened the door further. Lori's hair had darkened a bit, but otherwise, she looked the same, only much happier than the last time we got together.

"Take a seat." Lori pointed to the dining room table and chairs to the left. "I'm getting myself some coffee; do you want some?"

"Sure," I said as I sat down and looked around the apartment. It was large and neatly kept. Sunshine streamed in through the large living room window brightening the entire front area of the apartment. It felt happy here.

I heard a door open. "Are the kids here?"

"They're at school."

I glanced down the hall and saw a man walking toward me. "You must be Steve," I said rising to my feet. He stood about five foot ten and had a brownish-blonde trimmed beard and moustache, and very kind blue eyes. I extended my hand and said, "Hi Steve, I'm Bonny."

"Hi, Bonny. I feel like I already know you from everything Lori has told me," he said softly while he shook my hand. "Sit down." He turned to his wife, "Hon, would you get me a cup too?"

"Sure." Lori carried three filled coffee cups and joined us at the table. "I asked Steve to come home early today so he could meet you," she said.

"Wow, I feel honored. I hope you don't get in too much trouble for that, Steve."

"Nah, it's okay," he said.

Steve impressed me as a very quiet man, both in volume and in quantity of words spoken. But with Lori and me gabbing nonstop, the poor guy couldn't get a word in if he tried! His love for Lori was very evident from the way he looked at her and how he would touch her shoulder or place his hand over hers as we sat there at the table. I was thrilled for both of them—especially for Lori.

"Hey, Bonny," Lori said as she took our coffee cups and placed them in the sink. "Steve bought a little house out in the country. It's not much of a place right now, but I'd love to show it to you. Do you have time to go see it?"

I had a few hours before I needed to get ready for the reunion, so I agreed.

"I'll go pick up the kids," Steve said, "so you two have more time together."

What a sweet guy, I thought.

"Thanks, hon," Lori said before kissing Steve goodbye. "Well, let's go, Bonny."

Lori didn't enjoy driving, so we ended up taking my rental car: a silver Ford Mustang convertible. We lowered the top then drove out past the bar by the river we use to frequent to a two-lane country road. Soon more cornstalks and trees surrounded us than houses. I began to wonder how much farther we needed to travel, when Lori said "Turn left here, Bon." I obeyed. "Stop, there's the house!" Lori said pointing to a very small, weather-beaten wooden building. "I know it's not much now, but it will be!" She opened up her door, "Come on, let's get out and walk around." Lori's enthusiasm was contagious, so despite what my eyes saw, I followed her to the small building.

Lori shared her and Steve's plans for the little shell of a house. Steve planned on doing all the construction, electrical and plumbing work himself. Lori would do the interior decorating and landscaping. We walked around the acre lot. The narrow width allowed just enough room for the house, and maybe a double garage. However, the length of the lot stretched on and on. Tall pine trees bordered the west side of the yard. "Those trees will help protect the house from the bad weather that usually rolls in from the West." I nodded in agreement as we continued walking the length of the yard. It reached all the way south to the elementary school. After several minutes, we reached the schoolyard and sat a moment on the swings. "This will be great for the kids," Lori said. "They can walk to school and I can watch them all the way from our house to make sure they're safe. Isn't that great?" I'd never seen Lori so animated about something.

We walked back to the plywood-covered shelter and stepped inside. The building could not have been larger than eight-hundred square feet and was completely bare except for the plywood walls. It would take a lot of work to make this into a home that was livable.

"Lori, has Steve ever built a house before?" I asked. I didn't see how one person could do the plumbing, the electricity, the roofing and everything else this place needed. She was so excited, I would hate for Lori's dream to be shattered. She'd already suffered so many disappointments in her life.

"He's a construction superintendent, Bon. He does it everyday."

"Is he personally going to do the electrical and plumbing work?" I asked.

"He, and maybe, one other guy. He's confident he can do it."

I had my doubts, but decided not to burst Lori's bubble, so I dropped the questioning.

Lori shared her dreams about the flooring, the colors, the curtains and the counters for the house as we walked from area to area. She had thought about everything. This was her and Steve's little nest home, something she had dreamed about all her life.

14
SURPRISE

Within months of returning from the high school reunion, my luck seemed to have run out.

"Hey, Lor, I think I'm going to move back to Michigan."

"Oh, that's wonderful!" she said. "But, I thought you liked California?"

"Yeah, it's okay. But, when I went into work yesterday, I was called into a room and told my services were no longer needed," I said while letting Mew outside. "So I'm unemployed."

"I really want you to come home, but can't you get another job there?"

"I guess I could, but I don't really have close friends here, and don't really want to stay."

"What about Mr. Wonderful? Last thing you told me he was coming down there. Did he come?"

"Yeah, he came, briefly." I looked out and saw my cat sitting on the deck intently watching some birds. "He had been in town for four days before he even bothered to call me. We finally met at a coffee shop." The birds flew off and I walked over to let Mew back inside. "That's when he told me he was getting married—to someone else."

"What? Oh, Bon . . . what happened?"

The familiar tightness in my stomach started as I thought about that day. "He said he went out one night, ran into old friends, and there was this girl and they both felt electricity like they'd never felt before."

"Wow."

"Yeah, I'll get over it, but . . ." I stopped to light a cigarette. "It hurts, Lori. My stomach feels like he jabbed a knife in and twisted it. I *really* thought we'd get married. He smashed my dreams."

Lori sat silent for a moment and I continued to smoke my cigarette. "So that's why you're really leaving—to make a fresh start. Is that it?" she asked.

"You know me too well. Yes."

"Okay, you need to do what is right for you."

"I want to come home and lick my wounds."

"But, I know you loved Texas. Why not go back there?"

"Because . . . I need to be loved. You and my dad are in Michigan. I want to come home."

"And, you know, I want you here." As usual, Lori's words had helped to ease my tension. "So when are you leaving?"

"I'm shipping my belongings to my dad tomorrow, and then the next day I start driving. I think it will be a slow drive, since it's wintertime and I'm going to have to take the southern route. I haven't driven in snow for a long time."

"Well, you take your time and arrive in one piece. I'm so glad you're coming home, Bon. I've really missed you."

"I miss you too. I'll see ya soon."

 CREWS

During my time in Monterey, I met Antin at a beach party. He had a strong presence about him and was an incredibly attractive Native American with darkly tanned skin, black eyes, and long, thick, wavy black hair. We talked a long time that evening and since then we had run into each other several times at other parties.

A few weeks before I planned to leave, I ran into him again at a party and told him my news.

"That's interesting. I'm also leaving. I'm going back home to Taos, New Mexico to stay with my grandmother."

I had heard about Taos as an art community, but that's all I knew. "Is Taos a large city?"

Antin smiled, his teeth, although crooked, were very white against his tanned skin. "No, it's a small town. The Taos Pueblo is there."

I had learned about pueblos in my social studies class during seventh grade and had always been intrigued. It'd be interesting to see this place. I asked him more about Taos.

By the end of the party, we agreed to follow each other as far as New Mexico. After that, I'd be on my own.

With the rest of my belongings safely on a truck headed to Michigan, I loaded Mew and one suitcase into my tiny Fiat X19. I climbed into my car to wait for Antin. I could barely see the end of my car's hood through the thick morning fog that socked in the Monterey Peninsula.

I jumped when Antin rapped at my car's window. I hadn't seen him approach through the fog. I rolled down the window and said, "Hi, Are you ready?"

"Yes. Keep your low-beam headlights on until we get out of this fog. It shouldn't take long," he said before walking back to his car.

"I won't miss this," I said to Mew as I started the engine. A few hours into the trip, as we traveled east through the snow-covered mountains on Interstate 40, the temperature dropped drastically. The car's heater stopped working and my cat cuddled on my lap, keeping us both warm. Once the sun dipped behind the horizon, it began to snow and the wet roads soon became ice-covered death traps. I slowed my little blue car down to a crawl. Antin slowed down to stay behind me. We approached one large mountain and began the ascent. I needed to downshift to first gear just to keep the car moving forward. The engine began to overheat but the car made it to the top. In the illumination from my headlights I saw we were heading downhill once again. About halfway down the mountainside, without much weight, my car started to slide sideways. My heart raced as I fought to prevent us from sliding off the edge of the mountain. I remembered my old Michigan driver training days, *turn into the skid,* and with that, I brought the car under control but my knuckles were white with fear. *I have to stop.* The snowfall tapered and off in the distance I saw lights. "Hopefully it's a town with a motel," I said as I stroked Mew's back.

The lights turned out to be Flagstaff, Arizona. We found a little fleabag motel to get some rest. Antin left to go eat. After feeding Mew, I sprawled across the bed. My nerves were shot and I was exhausted. Within minutes, I fell sound asleep.

The next morning, the bright sunshine reflected off the snow-covered ground and the sky was a deep blue without a cloud in sight. I thought it would be a great day to travel. I felt refreshed and eager to hit the road.

Antin and I both climbed into our cars, but when I turned my key in the ignition, nothing happened. The car was completely dead. My friend came over and tried his luck. Still nothing. Together we walked to an auto shop a block away. A mechanic helped us, but diagnosed the engine as severely damaged and said the car couldn't be driven without major repairs. I had no choice but to leave my car at the shop, and hopefully, return one day to retrieve it. In the meantime, I needed to find a way home. Without credit cards and limited cash, that left few options. Thankfully, Antin agreed to give me, my cat and my suitcase a lift to New Mexico.

Late that evening we pulled into Antin's grandmother's yard and parked the car next to her house. It appeared to be constructed of mud and straw spread over chicken wire, as some of the chicken wire was exposed. Antin led me through the back opening into a kitchen. A large old metal woodstove, resting on woodblocks over the room's dirt floor, blasted heat into the room.

A short, but wide woman, with dark hair entered the room with her arms extended and a huge smile on her face that exposed her missing teeth. Antin bent over to hug and kiss her before he straightened up and pointed at me, saying something in a foreign tongue.

When I heard my name, I stepped forward with my hand extended and smiled. The smile on the woman's face vanished as she looked me over and ignored my hand. I looked at Antin, wondering what I had done wrong.

"This is my grandmother," he said. "She doesn't speak English, so I'll serve as interpreter." But, even I didn't need an interpreter to know she didn't like me. I could see the hatred flashing in her eyes when she said something to Antin, spitting out the word *gringo*. Antin conversed with her in a language similar to Spanish but mixed with the woman's native Indian language then he turned to me.

"I'm really sorry, but she doesn't want you to stay here. I have convinced her to let you stay tonight, since it's so late, but tomorrow you will need to leave."

I needed to work things out fast. I asked Antin if he'd take me to a gas station so I could make some phone calls. He turned and spoke to the woman. She said something while she kept her eyes on me. "Grandmother said you can use the phone here."

Surprised, I looked up at Antin. "I can? There's a phone?" Based on what I'd seen of the kitchen, I didn't think there would be.

"Yes, the rest of the house is modern. Follow me."

As Antin had said, there was flooring, electricity and plumbing in other parts of the adobe home. He handed me the phone. "Just don't be on it too long, or she'll get angry."

I nodded my head, "Thanks, Antin." I quickly called my father collect and two other Saginaw friends who I thought might help. No luck. Then I called a friend from Austin who agreed to come get me.

I made one last collect call. "Lor," I said through a crackling phone line.

"Bon, Bonny is that you?"

"Yeah, Lor. Hey, listen I can't talk long. My car broke down, I'm not making it home. The only place I can get to is Austin, so that's where I'm heading. A friend is coming here to pick me up. I'll call you when I get settled. I gotta go. Love you."

I'm sure my call drove Lori nuts; but I didn't want to antagonize my friend's grandmother. That night I slept curled up in a chair, holding my cat and the next evening, my friend from Texas arrived to take me back to his home.

CRE80

After four weeks back in Austin, I found an efficiency apartment on the bus line. My father told me it was too expensive to ship my belongings to me, so I slowly obtained clothing, furnishings and supplies through rummage sales and Goodwill.

"Hey, Lor. Long time no talk!"

"Bonny! Man, I've been worried about you after that last call. Are you okay? Did you make it to Texas?"

After giving Lori my address and describing my new apartment, I said, "Hey Lor, remember that time under the 'Umbrella Tree' when you told me about the abortion case?"

"Yeah. Why? Are you pregnant?"

I laughed. "By who?" I laughed again. "No, I'm not pregnant, but I am working as a secretary with an attorney who was married to the lawyer who won the right to have an abortion—that Roe vs. Wade case."

"Wow, that's cool."

"It is cool, Lori. The law firm I work at is small, but everyone there is *somebody*. Attorneys and politicians I'd heard about and even seen on TV and now I'm working side-by-side with them. It's so interesting to spend lunch in the kitchen with them as they discuss cases, politics and talk about things around town. Sometimes we even watch *All My Children* together. It's hilarious when our town's former mayor is telling

Erica to dump whoever. We all laugh a lot. It's so fun, Lori!" I switched the phone to the other ear and then asked, "So what's up in your world?"

"Oh, not much. I'm always busy it seems with the kids and Steve's kids. We're all going camping this weekend, so today I'm busy preparing for that." Lori paused. I could hear her exhale cigarette smoke. "We had dinner the other night with Steve's ex and her husband."

I wondered if I heard that right. "You did? Wasn't that awkward?"

"Yes we did, and no, not weird. I really like his ex. She's a good person."

"That's wild, Lori. I'm sure not many women become friends with their spouse's ex. But, then again, it's you, and you always seem to find the good in everyone. We should all try to be more like you"

"Oh, Bon. I'm not anything special. Cut it out."

"Well, I think you're great, Lor, and I'm happy your life is filled with others who love you."

"I love being around my family, but seriously it's pretty mundane compared to your life. Working where you do and the things you've done. You should write a book!"

"Yeah, right."

I heard voices on Lori's end. "Hon," she said, "I've got to run. The kids are back from school and I've got to pack. Love you!"

It took a few months, but eventually I'd saved enough to purchase a car: an unpainted, badly worn 1970 Ford Mustang. The engine worked; pretty much everything else was shot. During my free time I spray painted the car white, added black pin-striping, went to the junk yard to purchase a front grill, headlight covers, hubcaps and other parts that were missing. I even sewed the red headliner by hand. I was proud of what I'd accomplished, but even though I had a car that ran, and it didn't look too bad, I continued riding the bus to conserve money. My next goal: purchase a house within two years.

ଔଡ଼ୠ

A long list of HUD homes for sale appeared on the back page of the newspaper each Friday. With the help of an excellent real estate broker I met, I started looking and finally found one.

Because the house had stood vacant for two years, when my offer came in for just one-third of what it had been valued at before the Savings and Loan crisis of 1986, it was accepted.

The small limestone ranch house had two bedrooms and one bathroom, and was located on the edge of town with a view of fields that spanned to the horizon. The house needed work, but rather than seeing it as it stood, I saw what it could be.

If everything continued moving according to schedule, the house would be mine the Monday after Thanksgiving. Since my house payments were going to be less than the rent on the small efficiency apartment I'd lived in for the past two years, my days of eating cheap noodles and riding the bus would soon be coming to an end. I had to share my news with Lori.

"Hey, Lor, guess what!"

"Hi, Bon, what?"

"I'm buying a house!"

"Yeah? Tell me about it."

I described the floor plan and then said, "It's on the edge of the countryside, so I have cows across the street, but as long as the wind doesn't come from the south, I really like it!"

Lori laughed. "You're such an animal-lover, I don't think the smell of cow manure would bother you too much." I could hear her take a drag on a cigarette. Nonchalantly Lori said, "We moved into our house."

"Lori, that's so exciting! So is it all done?"

"No, not really. Every time we think we're almost there, we find something or realize we need to do something else, and everything seems to take longer than we originally planned. But you know . . ."

"What?"

"I don't mind. We're in our own home, and I'm thrilled."

CR&O

Just days before closing on my house, I got up like any other day, letting Mew out while I got my morning coffee brewing. As I poured my first cup, Mew screamed louder than I'd ever heard him. I raced to the front door. I looked out and saw two dogs, a large Akita and a Bull Terrier, had pinned Mew upside down to the ground with their mouths.

I yelled, "Hey! What are you doing?" A thought crossed my mind to grab a broom and throw on a bathrobe, but I ignored it as I flew down the stairs to Mew's rescue. The dogs looked up, releasing my cat. He scrambled underneath the nearest car in the parking lot. As I reached the bottom of the stairs, the Bull Terrier ran around the car where Mew hid, but the Akita lunged at me, digging his teeth into my right arm, violently twisting it, trying to rip it of my body.

With more surprise than pain, I shouted, "Ow!" I had not expected the dog to attack me and tried to keep calm, until the pain set in. I had to fight back to protect myself.

The Akita continued tearing at my arm, which by now, was going numb. Blood flowed off my fingertips onto the dog and the ground. I screamed in pain, *"HELP! Somebody HELP ME!"*

Just as suddenly as the dog had attacked, he released my arm. I began running, but from the corner of my eye, I saw the dog leap at me. In a protective reflex, I cringed up my shoulders just as the dog's powerful jaws wrapped around the back of my head and neck, narrowly missing my jugular vein.

The dog lifted me off the ground and whipped me back and forth, as if I were a rag doll. I used the elbow of my injured arm to blindly jab the head of the dog behind me, over and over and over again; all the while hysterically crying at the top of my lungs, *"HELP! MY GOD, SOMEBODY HELP ME!"* My strength drained as my blood sprayed everywhere with each blow to the dog's forehead. Still nobody came to my rescue.

With the force of desperation, I smashed the dog between the eyes with my elbow one last time. The dog yelped in pain and dropped me abruptly to my knees on the rough asphalt. The dog ran off.

I struggled to lift my head, but I was too weak.

Despite the bright sunshine, an eerie quietness prevailed. Not even a bird chirped. I looked at the blood-covered asphalt—my blood. Using my good arm, I slowly pushed myself up then looked closely at my injured arm where the skin was ripped away, exposing the muscle and watched blood seep out. *Oh my God! I've got to get help or I just might really die.*

The nearest apartment belonged to my downstairs neighbor. *I need to make it to that door.* With all the energy I could muster, I slowly stood up. A wave of dizziness overtook me and I braced myself against the nearest car. When the dizziness passed, in a bent over position, I inched my way to the door.

Leaning against the door, I heard low music inside. I turned and saw a trail of blood from the parking lot to where I stood. Looking down, I noticed a puddle of blood forming at my feet. With my head against the door, I hit it repeatedly with my open palm.

Finally, a young man cracked open the door. He seemed to be around twenty-five years old wearing only boxer shorts and it appeared he had just woken up. The young man left the door chain secured while he stared at me.

Annoyance showed on his face when he noticed the bloody palm prints I had left on his door. "It's the crack of dawn. What do you want?"

Breathlessly I answered, "Help . . . me. Call 9-1-1. Dogs . . . attacked . . . me."

The man looked me over slowly, head to toe, and then returned his glare to the blood on his door. "I don't want to get involved," he said coldly, and with that, closed the door in my face.

Dumbfounded, I leaned back against the closed door, slowly shaking my head. *How can a person turn away from someone so obviously in need of help?* Tears welled up as a growing feeling of utter disbelief and devastation filled me, but I fought the urge to give up.

I slowly turned around and looked up the stairs to my apartment. *I can do this!* I grabbed a hold of the railing with my good arm and slowly ascended the stairs, stopping every few steps to breathe and gather energy.

Although exhausted, through sheer determination I reached my open door. *Made it!* Hunched over, I staggered to the phone, grabbed it, stepped back outside, dialed 9-1-1, then leaned against the doorframe for support.

As the operator asked for my address, I looked up and saw the two dogs with Mew swaying between their mouths. "Trace . . . the call . . . ," I said before dropping the phone.

With strength I didn't know I possessed, I yelled, "Mew, I love you!"

At the sound of my voice, he lifted his head and looked directly at me, then his head dropped as his final breath flowed out of his body.

"N-O-O-O-O-O-O-O!" I screamed as an ambulance and squad car raced around the corner. Two officers jumped out. The dogs dropped the lifeless cat and charged them. After several rounds of ammunition, the dogs fell dead in the parking lot.

Before being taken away in the ambulance, I asked an officer to put Mew in my bathtub, so I could bury him later.

While I was in the hospital, one of the attorneys I worked for handled the closing on my new home.

Upon release from the hospital, a friend helped me bury Mew in the backyard of my new home. Then I began packing up my apartment as best as I could with the use of only one arm.

In the closet, I came across some of Mew's toys he had hidden. "God, why did you take Mew away?" Tears flowed down my face, sobs racked my body, as I sat on my folded legs, rocking and holding Mew's catnip mouse to my chest. "He's all I had."

I dried my tears and forced myself to continue packing. I picked up a box to carry down to my car, put it in my trunk and turned to go back upstairs to get yet another box, when I noticed a little jet-black kitten with greenish-gold eyes watching me from underneath a bush. It couldn't have been more than twelve weeks old. I briefly wondered who the kitten belonged to. I knelt down and extended my finger for the kitten to sniff. "Hi Kitty." The kitten sniffed my finger. "Aren't you precious?" I said as I tried to pet the kitten, but it backed away so I continued back upstairs for another box.

When I started down the stairs with the next box, a young woman stood outside talking to the kitten. "Hi. Is that your kitten?" I asked her.

She stood up. "Yes, one of five kittens. My cat had them and I'm trying to find them homes."

I reached the bottom of the stairs and looked at the kitten who sat watching both of us. "It sure is cute," I said.

"Would you like her?"

I looked at the woman and then at the kitten. My heart fluttered with excitement. "Really?"

"Yes, like I said, I need to find them homes."

I reached out to the kitten who rubbed her head against my fingers. "Wow, you don't know how much this means to me. I recently lost my cat, and this is like an answer to my prayer." I looked back at the woman. "Yes, I'd love to have this kitten. Thank you so much!"

After a few minutes of building the kitten's trust, I picked her up, took her upstairs then sat down on the couch and petted her. "Welcome home, Inky."

The next day Inky and I moved into our new home and I called Lori to tell her of the drama I'd recently survived, and Mew didn't.

CR80

It took three months of physical therapy before I finally regained full use of my damaged arm and was able to type and return to work.

During the weekends, I planted dozens of bushes around the perimeter of the back yard and a few trees in front of my new home. Inky helped by digging and rolling in the piles of dirt. I also painted all the interior walls, and in the attic, I laid insulation and installed a floor for storage space. No matter what I was working on, Inky stayed closed to my side "supervising."

CR80

Over the next year Lori and I stayed in contact by phone on a monthly basis. Her news always revolved around the people she loved: her kids, stepkids, husband and her mother and siblings and their kids. She also always gave me updates on Saginaw and the people we knew.

I continued working at the law firm, but didn't receive a raise and without any insurance, I decided it was time to make a change. A little over a year after moving into my home, my ability to type over one hundred words per minute landed me a word-processing job in 1991 at a scientific research firm. It paid nearly double what I had been earning at the law firm and the employees I spent my days with were intelligent, interesting and fun to be with. Once a week, the entire department would get together after the workday to alleviate stress by playing volleyball. Many times, we also held *weisers*—a keg of Budweiser to be enjoyed by all—in conjunction with the games. The group I worked with soon became very close friends, especially one of the chemical engineers.

"Hey, Lori, I've got news."

"Yeah . . . have you finally met the man of your dreams?"

"Well, I've met someone."

"Yeah, tell me all about him. How'd you meet? What does he look like? Are you getting married?" Lori asked.

"We met at work. No wedding bells . . . we just met . . . and he's not my type, for sure. Definitely not what I envisioned as 'the man of my dreams.' He's tall, I'm short. I'm sure we look like Mutt and Jeff standing next to each other." Lori laughed. "He's Scandinavian, super pale, white blond hair, light blue eyes, big boned. His legs are too skinny, he's going bald . . . but I love his sense of humor. He's the only person on this earth, besides my brother, who can make me laugh until I cry. But enough about me, what about you?"

"Does he have a name?"

I laughed. "Forgot that part, didn't I? His name is Jim."

"I'm so happy for you! As far as me . . ." I heard Lori light up a smoke, and take a drag before she continued, "both kids are doing well in school and I'm enjoying helping them with their work and I bake cookies and stuff for special events. Steve is working hard and staying busy. Overall life is good."

"You're a little 'Suzy Homemaker'! So, exactly opposite from me. I mean, I burn water. Cooking is just not my thing."

Lori laughed. "Hey, Bon, your dad is in insurance right?"

"Yeah. Actually, he's an adjuster. Why? Did you guys get in an accident or was your house broken into?"

"No, no, nothing like that. Steve and I have been talking and we're going to get some life insurance and wondered what you suggested."

"Lor, not my thing. My grandfather sold life insurance. Of course, he's gone now. I do remember him telling me *whole* life is better than *term* because it builds up value. Whole life is like owning a home, while term life is like renting it. My dad might be able to help you."

"Okay and th—" suddenly loud children's voices were heard. "Hey, Bon, kids are home, I've got to run. Love ya!"

⋙⋘

Gaps between our phone calls increased, but Lori and I always picked up wherever we left off. One weekend a few years later, I called to catch up.

"So, Bon, are you ever going to settle down? Don't you want to have kids?"

"Well, Jim and I are still dating."

"Yeah . . . and?"

"We've taken a few vacations together to New Orleans and Kiawah Island."

"Yeah . . . and?"

"He comes over nearly every day and we usually hang out until I need to get some sleep."

"Yeah . . . and?"

"I'd love to get married, Lori. He said he wants to marry me, but he always has a million excuses why he can't set a date."

"Uh-oh."

"Yeah, and I'm beginning to get *very* frustrated. I'm in my mid-thirties now, and I sure hope I'm not wasting my time with him. The pickins' out there have really dried up. And as far as kids, I wonder if I would even be able to get pregnant, and if I did, I'd worry about the health of the baby; my eggs are getting pretty old!"

"You're not *that* old," Lori laughed. "So what are his excuses?"

"Oh, they change daily. Lor, I think he's just stringing me along and has no intention of marrying me. What do you think?"

"Well, I don't know him. I can only go on what you've told me. Honestly, if he wanted to marry you, why would he be making excuses? He's getting the milk without buying the cow."

"Yeah, I think you're right." Her words crushed me. I needed to break up with him before all the straight attractive men were taken. "So what's up with you, Lor?"

"Well, you know Marie has started high school."

"Oh my gosh! It seems like just yesterday she was this little girl playing mommy to her baby brother."

"Yeah, I know," Lori said. "Before you know it, she'll be graduating from high school, and that's got me thinking."

"Thinking about what, Lor?"

"I think it's time I got my high school diploma."

"Oh, Lor, *Yes*! It will change your life and bring more opportunities to you. And, you'll feel proud of yourself. Do it!" I said.

"I'm thinking about it. The high school near here offers an adult program at night so I would actually earn a diploma, rather than just a GED certificate."

"Do it, Lor. Don't think about it, just do it!"

"Maybe . . ."

Over the next several months, I'd call and give Lori updates, and she'd give me updates on her life. Though we lived so far apart physically, our friendship remained as close as ever.

CR₰

"I'm so glad you answered, Lor I really need your advice." I said on one of our many calls.

"About what?"

"First, tell me, how's school going?" Lori had started her one-year program a few months earlier.

"It's going great! I'm pulling straight A's and really enjoying it. I'll graduate in June. Maybe you can come?" Lori asked.

"Well, it depends on some things."

"Like what? Is that what you wanted to talk about?"

"Yeah," I paused to prepare for the announcement, "Lor, it happened."

"What?"

"I'm pregnant."

"Yeah? Are you happy about it?"

Forgetting all about my vow as a teenager not to have children, I said, "I'm thrilled. I'll be thirty-six by the time the baby is born. But, *he* wants me to get an abortion—and refuses to marry me."

"What do you want?"

"To do things the right way."

"Bon, you told me once a very long time ago to follow my heart . . . and now I'm telling you."

"My heart, gut, soul are screaming to have this baby, but my head is arguing saying 'but you're not married'; 'how can you afford a baby?'; 'you'll be disowned by the family'; and blah, blah, blah." I took a deep breath and exhaled slowly. "Lor, I'm scared."

"Do you remember how scared I was when I found out I was pregnant with Marie?"

"Yeah, but at least her father came through for you and wanted you to have her," I pointed out.

"Uh-huh . . . and look how that turned out."

"Right."

"The only reason you're scared is because you don't know what the future holds. But think about this, if you live your life to please others and you end up never having another chance to have a baby, will you regret it?"

I answered without hesitation. "Yes."

"Follow your heart."

CR£O

The months sped by. The day Lori called, I felt like a giant blob.

"Bon, how are you doing?"

"I feel like I'm ready to explode. I'm five feet tall and five feet wide and still have three more months to go!"

Lori giggled at my description. "I guess this means you don't feel like traveling home to come to my graduation."

"Oh, Lor! When is it?"

"In three weeks."

"I can't. I'm too fat to drive the car that far, and I don't want to fly right now; it might hurt the baby."

"I understand." Lori's pitch dropped with disappointment.

"I'm sorry, Lor, but I'll be there with you in spirit. Please have someone take lots of photos so I can see you in your cap and gown, okay?"

Although I couldn't be there, I thought of Lori that day, so happy she had accomplished the goals, one by one, she had so long ago put down on paper.

"Congrats, High School Graduate! So, how did it go, Lori? Tell me all about it."

"I was so scared and nervous. I was literally shaking as I got dressed in my cap and gown."

"Why were you nervous?"

"You know, at first I had no idea, but I think I figured it out. I thought about the crowd, but that wasn't it. I thought about my family sitting there in the audience supporting me, but that wasn't it either. I finally figured it out when the principal actually handed me that hard-earned piece of paper. I guess I didn't really believe my dream would ever come true, and was waiting for something to destroy it. But, that didn't happen. When I held that diploma," Lori paused for a moment, "Well, now I know dreams do come true."

"I'm so proud of you, Lor."

"Thanks, Bon. I don't want this to sound vain, but I'm pretty proud of myself too! At long last, I'm finally a high school graduate."

CREED

Two months after Lori's graduation, the day began as any other Saturday. I went to my Lamaze class, watched my friends play a game of volleyball, then came home and vacuumed and did the dishes. That evening, not really tired, I climbed on my bed and leaned back against the pillows, then placed a book on my belly and began reading.

After several minutes, I realized I'd been reading and rereading the same paragraph. I couldn't focus on the book. *I might as well get up.*

I waddled into the kitchen, looked into the refrigerator but nothing looked good. Then I made my way into the living room and carefully lowered myself onto the rocking chair.

After a few minutes, I grew very uncomfortable. *What was going on?* I pushed myself out of the chair and walked back toward the bedroom when I felt water dribbling down my leg. *Crap,* I thought, *wetting my pants again. I can't wait for this baby to be born, so I can control my bladder!*

But this time, the dribble turned into a geyser. My water had broken—and I was home all alone. The baby's father was out of town on business. My backup coach was off camping with her fiancé and couldn't be reached. I called my doctor. She was not on call. A doctor I'd never met would be waiting for me.

I grabbed my "focus" creature—a dark-brown, three-foot-tall stuffed gorilla I named Mr. Godfrey Aloysius Gorilla, but I called him Mr. Gag. I strapped him in the passenger seat, then squeezed my big self into my little Mazda RX7 and began driving to the hospital just four miles away.

I looked down at the gas indicator: empty. *Perfect.* I headed to the nearest 7-11, hoping I had enough gas to make it there. Thankfully, I did. With great effort, I pried myself out of the car.

Just as I stuck the gas nozzle into my gas tank opening, an overpowering pain wracked my body. *"Breathe!"* I said through clenched teeth. A moment later the pain was gone. *Wow. That must have been a labor pain. I need to get to the hospital now so I can get drugs and not have to feel that again!*

I squeezed the lever to pump gas into my car then looked up at the pump and saw a man standing on the other side. He stared at me with his mouth hanging open, obviously inebriated. "It's okay," I told him. "I'm having a baby, but I will try not to have it here." He snapped his mouth shut but continued watching me as I finished putting three gallons of gas in my car, squeezed myself back into the driver's seat then continued on to the hospital. I wondered if the drunk would even remember. Probably not.

When I arrived at the hospital, an orderly came running out pushing a wheelchair to collect Mr. Gag and me. It was one-thirty in the morning. After a quick sonogram, the doctor advised me I had a son but the baby was not properly positioned for delivery.

"No, it's a thumb; I really believe it's a girl."

"We don't have time to debate the issue," the doctor said. "The baby is breech and you need to undergo an emergency C-section."

A nurse standing nearby said, "I'll go get the gurney now."

As I lay there waiting, another contraction took over. I dealt with that as I deal with all things too painful: shift focus to something good and sweet. I thought about this little baby in my arms. Saw her running through a flowery field on a sunny day, with her hair flying behind her. I didn't notice when the pain left.

"Smiling like that, you must be feeling pretty good," the nurse said as she and another worker placed me on the gurney.

"I was concentrating on something besides the here and now."

Within minutes of being ushered into the operating room, someone injected a large needle into the base of my spine. I hated needles and shots, but I couldn't see it, so after the initial prick, I didn't mind the needle there. A warm numbness began to spread throughout my body and soon I didn't feel anything. *No more labor pains, yeah!*

As I lay on my back on a metal table in a sterile room flooded in bright lights, doctors and nurses moved quickly around me to prepare for the surgery. Shortly after setting up a white curtain just below my shoulders to block my view of the delivery, I heard the doctor slit the skin of my stomach.

At that moment, I wished I had a loving husband to be there with me. I wanted someone to hold my hand and share this moment. Instead, I found myself surrounded by complete strangers. The thought brought tears to my eyes. I closed my eyes and told myself, *Enough of this pity party! Change your thoughts, now.* I opened my eyes and saw Mr. Gag sitting off to the side. That only reinforced how alone I was, that I had to bring a stuffed animal because my baby's father, my coach, not even my doctor were with me at this moment.

I looked to my side where a person sat monitoring a machine with my stats. "Hey, have you heard any good jokes lately?" I asked.

The man looked up at me and smiled, then reverted his eyes back to the screen. Obviously, he didn't think I really wanted to hear jokes.

"So have you?"

"No, not really."

"Well, then I've got some for you," and I began telling several jokes to everyone in the room until I felt a mild tug deep within my body. I stopped talking, and within seconds, I heard a baby's cry in rebellion to being removed from the warm secure cocoon that had been home for the past nine months. It was 3:20 in the morning—and my whole world had changed forever.

"Is it a girl?" I looked directly into the doctor's eyes.

"Yes."

"Told you so!" I said with a smile. "Is she okay?"

"She looks wonderful, nice and pink. Would you like to see her?"

"Yes," I said, but just as the doctor stood in front of me holding my newborn daughter, I suddenly had an overwhelming urge to vomit—and I did—violently, all over both of them.

What a baptism.

In less than twenty-four hours after giving birth via an emergency C-section, with nobody at home to help me, the hospital personnel rushed me out saying they needed the beds. Thankfully, Ann, my birthing coach, was back from camping and drove my daughter, Jennifer, and me home.

Inky greeted us at the door. Jennifer, who was fast asleep and swaddled up in warm blankets, didn't notice Inky, but Inky was on full alert wondering what this strange thing was. She sniffed the air around her, hissed, and then promptly left the room. She obviously didn't like this new object in the house.

Ann gently placed Jennifer in her bassinet next to my bed, and then helped settle me into my bed. My stomach was stapled shut from the C-section, and I wasn't supposed to be moving around much. Ann had offered to stay with me for a few days to help, but she needed to run home and get some clothes, so she left.

I lay in bed with my head turned so I could admire this little person sleeping so peacefully next to me. So innocent, so sweet. After a few moments, I rolled my head and looked up, unseeing, at the off-white popcorn ceiling and thought, *No husband; no family. We were alone. Not what I had envisioned for the homecoming of my daughter.*

CЯ℘

"Hey Lor." Ann had stayed three days, showing me how to do things, but she had to get back to work. She had been a pure blessing and after great debate, I had come to a decision.

"Bonny! Did you have the baby?"

"Yes. It's a girl. She's seven pounds, fourteen ounces, twenty-one inches with a full head of black hair and deep blue/black eyes. Her eyes will probably turn dark brown. I named her Jennifer."

"Oh congratulations, Bonny! I love that name."

"Lori, I wanted you to be her godmother, but the other day I was lying in bed and realized if anything happens to me, Jennifer will be an orphan. I know just the thought of traveling any length of time in cars, buses, planes or trains makes you feel claustrophobic. So, if something happened to me, how would you make the trip to Texas?"

"Bonny, nothing is going to happen to you."

"Well, I hope not, but if it does . . . Lor, I hope you don't hate me, but I decided to make Ann, a good friend of mine who lives here, Jennifer's godmother. Please don't hate me." I really hoped my decision would not deeply hurt Lori. If we lived closer to each other, it would have been her and I told her as much.

"Bon, I understand and it's okay with me." Relief washed over me.

Lori and I talked a little longer and then I called my father.

"Dad, I had the baby. Will you please come down to help me and to meet your granddaughter?" He gave me every excuse in the book why he couldn't. "Let me talk to Angie."

"Why?"

"Maybe your wife will come. I need help." Father reluctantly handed the phone to Angie.

"Hello, Angie."

"Hi, Bonny, how are you feeling?"

"Overwhelmed, sore." I took a breath and then went full throttle. "I need help, Angie. Would you be willing to come to Texas and stay with me for a week to help? I know I'm asking a lot, but my mom can't help since she resides in heaven, and as I'm sure you just heard, my father refuses, so I'm *really* hoping you can come. I think it would give us some time to get to know each other better as well. Will you come?"

"I've never been to Austin."

"You might enjoy it. It's a little warm, but I have a small aboveground pool. I'll help pay for a plane ticket."

"No, you don't have to do that. I'll come. I'll drive down."

"Thanks, Angie. This really means the world to me. Thank you."

I was furious at my father for caring so little about his first (and it turned out only) grandchild. Suddenly I saw his wife in a new light. I looked forward to her visit.

CRSO

A few days later, the phone rang while Jennifer was sleeping. I grabbed the receiver before the second ring and answered with a whisper, "Hello?"

"Hey Bonny, this is Andrew. I recently moved back to Saginaw, and asked your dad for your number. Anyways, I'm calling to let you know I'm coming to Texas with some friends. I was hoping to stop by and see you."

"Andrew!" I stepped outside onto the covered patio so I could speak at a normal volume. "I'd love to see you. Things have changed a little with me, I just gave birth to a little girl."

"Yeah? Will your husband mind if we stop by?"

"No husband, long story better saved for another day. You know you are always welcome in my home. When will you be here?"

"Next week."

I began cleaning the house and preparing for the onslaught of visitors, as best as I could, eagerly anticipating their arrival.

As promised, Andrew stopped by with two of his friends. He looked and acted pretty much the same as he did in high school, except his hair was getting thinner on top and cut short in back. He still had a quick smile and a twinkle in his blue eyes. I really enjoyed seeing him again after all these years, and he adored my daughter, who slept throughout most of his visit. During the few hours that Andrew and his friends stayed, he told me he'd been living in Utah for several years, but his father had recently died, so he returned home to be near his mother. I brought him up to date with my life as well. It was a good visit.

The next day the doorbell chimed. There stood Angie—and Father—with big smiles on their faces.

"Dad! I thought you weren't coming."

"Yeah, well, it wouldn't have looked good if your stepmother came and your father didn't."

"The guilt got to him," Angie winked at me.

I smiled at her while I held the door open for them to enter. Angie had convinced Father to come, and I owed her eternal gratefulness.

They stayed with us for a week. We visited outlying small towns, wineries, downtown restaurants and the lake. Angie taught me tips for taking care of my baby and Father played the devoted grandpa carrying Jennifer in a papoose on his chest. As I had predicted, although Father and Angie had now been married nineteen years, this was the first time Angie and I finally got to really know each other and I liked her—a lot.

A few weeks after all the visitors had gone, I began to grow depressed from loneliness. Jennifer's father came by less and less. When he stopped over, it was usually for just a few minutes. If he stayed for an hour, I felt lucky. It was pathetic. I now knew with certainty that there was no future with this man. I loved him, but I had to get over it and him. The only way I could think of to do that was to leave. I wanted to go home, home to be near Lori and my father and stepmother. My priorities had shifted.

"Hey Lor," suddenly missing my best friend so much. "It's good to hear your voice."

"Bonny!"

I started crying. "Lori, I want to come home."

"Why, hon?"

"Maybe this is that postpartum blues, but I've finally realized Jennifer's father will never commit to us and I just want to be closer to my family, and you. I want my daughter to know her only grandparents."

"What about your house and job?"

"I'll sell the house. I can always get another job."

"Follow your heart, Bon," Lori wisely said. "Hey, speaking of jobs, I have a job!"

I dried my tears and focused on Lori's good fortune. "Really? That's awesome! What kind of work is it?"

"It's called *Boysville*, a home for juvenile delinquents, and I work in the cafeteria."

The job sounded ideal for Lori. She loved cooking, and because she had gone through so much in her past: the drinking, her first husband's drug habit and the welfare; she could relate very well with what these boys' lives were like. She could empathize and get them to open up, as she visited with them each day during their meals, to the real underlying issue—usually a feeling of being unloved resulting in bad behavior just to get attention.

"Hey Lor, maybe this was God's plan."

"What do you mean?" Lori asked somewhat confused.

"Well, with all the challenges and struggles you've endured, you've learned some valuable lessons, that you can now share to help those boys."

Lori downplayed anything special about herself, but I saw it clearly. Lori now had the ability to change the world, one boy at a time. It made sense now. Lori ended up working at *Boysville* for years.

15
HOME AGAIN

Nearly a year after my daughter's birth, a few friends helped me load up the rented full-sized U-haul truck and strap down my car on the attached trailer. After saying goodbye to them, I began the drive back to Michigan with my daughter and our growing family of cats. We now had four furry feline friends: Inky, Samantha, Mr. Bobbit and Tabitha.

The trip was long, but aside from the torrential downpour in Kentucky, we had an uneventful trip back to the town where I grew up. Andrew, who now managed his family's rental properties and visited his aging mother every day, helped me unload the U-Haul truck, along with two other guys. Once they left, I began setting up my new household. I felt very blessed to have such wonderful, helpful friends in two states.

I finally pulled into Lori's gravel driveway my third day after moving to town. She stood waiting outside for us. It was so good to see her again—it had been eleven years since I'd laid eyes on her. Her blonde hair now contained several strands of gray, she wore new glasses with gold-wired rims, and she'd put on a few pounds; but otherwise, still the same Lori I knew and loved. When we first saw each other, we just hugged and cried.

"God, I've missed you!" Lori said.

Being too choked up for words, "Ditto," is all I could respond with.

"Why cry, Mama?" Lori and I released each other to look down toward the innocent voice and smiled.

"She's adorable, Bonny."

"Thanks, Lor," I said as I picked up my little girl. Her black hair had fallen out and been replaced by white-blonde hair— just like her daddy's. We followed Lori into her home.

"Do you want some coffee?" she asked as we went into the kitchen she'd decorated with red roosters.

"Sure."

"I've been so busy around here!" Lori handed me a cup with steam rising from the ebony liquid. I took a sip then set it down to let it cool.

She took me on a tour of her home. Looking around the little house, it was a far cry from when I originally saw it. The place was adorable. The home had become what Lori and Steve had envisioned so many years before. Steve had done all the plumbing and electrical work, installed insulation, and put up interior walls. Lori had helped Steve install flooring, paint the walls and ceilings, hang wallpaper, and then she added her own touches by hanging curtains and decorations. "Come on outside, and see what we've done."

I picked up Jennifer from the floor of the living room and all three of us went outside. I set my daughter down, and in her unsteady waddle, she followed us around. Near the large trees in the backyard, Lori had planted a variety of flowers and vegetables producing a colorful garden of yellow, pink, red and white mixed in with leaves of green. "You did all this?"

"Yep. I love it. I love getting my hands dirty and watching these grow. It makes me feel good."

"Well, it's beautiful, Lor. You've done a great job! I like being outside and even playing in the dirt, but anything I touch turns brown. You've obviously got the touch!"

"Thanks. Now for the final touch."

I looked back at the house amazed at the transformation. Steve had put on a black roof, installed blue vinyl siding and added white shutters around the windows. He had built a wooden porch the width of the house in front and painted it white to match the shutters. Lori had planted flowers and shrubs around the home's perimeter. The place seemed perfect to me. "What final touch?"

"We're getting a pool! It's only an aboveground pool, but we'll be putting a deck around it, and I'm so excited. I think I missed not having a pool more than I realized," Lori said.

The little house was definitely a much-loved home now, thanks to the love both Lori and Steve had poured into it.

We went back inside to get another cup of coffee. We'd just sat down at the kitchen table, when the side door opened. Steve walked in from a long day at work. It surprised me to see Steve's beard and hair pure gray. But then, years had passed since I had seen him last. He had spent those years working to provide this home for Lori and the kids, to raise Marie and Ken as his own children, as well as be a father to his two children from his previous marriage. He had done a great job. The kids had grown up happy and knew they were loved.

"Hi Steve," I said wondering if he'd even recognize me. My hair was mousy brown again and I was twenty pounds heavier than the last time he saw me.

"Bonny! Lori said you were coming back. Welcome home."

"Thanks."

Steve kissed Lori on the cheek and then went to take a shower. I checked on Jennifer in the living room; she contentedly watched a Barney video.

"Steve looks good, though a bit older," I said as I sat back down at the kitchen table.

"Yeah, it happens to the best of us." Lori lit up a cigarette. "Did I tell you I completely stopped drinking?"

"No. When did you decide to do that?"

"Awhile ago. Steve wanted me to, and the kids don't deserve a drunk mom." A grin crept across her face. "I think someone told me that a long time ago."

I smiled in return. "I'm proud of you, Lor."

CRSO

I quickly found work at the largest radio station in the area selling advertising as well as writing and doing voice-overs for the ads. I loved it. The job provided the means for me to purchase a beautiful white colonial-style home built in 1940. It sat on a large lot with a huge backyard, bordered with pine trees that reached up about four stories tall. I bought it from the original owner and was very proud to call it my home.

CRSO

Winter weather gripped Michigan and the snow crunched under my boots as I carried Jennifer from the car to Lori's door. I rapped loudly before adjusting the soft beige knit scarf to block the icy wind from going down my throat.

Raising my daughter, single-handedly, and working full-time at the radio station left me little time for social visits, but I made it a point to visit Lori several times a month. I usually dropped by unannounced.

"Who is it?" I heard her yell through the door.

"Bonny and Jennifer."

"Oh, just a minute, hon."

I heard a sharp, yapping. *Was that a dog's bark?* I thought as I silently began to freeze waiting for Lori.

The door opened, and there she stood in her full-length velveteen blue robe. She held open the storm door to let us in.

"Sorry, I got a new little girl; her name is Maggie, and sometimes she bites, so I had to put her in the bathroom. How are you?" Lori said as we hugged hello.

"Dog?" my daughter asked excitedly in her little two-year-old voice, as we walked into the kitchen. "Can I pet her?"

Lori kneeled down to be at Jennifer's eye level. "Yes. I have a baby dog. She hasn't learned to be polite yet, which means she might bite you, and I wouldn't want you to get hurt."

Disappointment covered my baby's face.

"I'll tell you what, how about I go get Maggie, and hold her, and you can at least see her. Is that okay?"

My daughter nodded her head. A huge smile lit up her big deep-brown eyes.

Lori stood up and looked at me. "Make yourself at home, grab some coffee; I'll be right back."

A few moments later, Lori walked back into the room with this little fluff of gray and brown hair in the crook of her arm. She held a very small Yorkshire Terrier puppy. The tiny dog barked profusely at us, growled and showed her tiny teeth. "This is my new baby, her name is Maggie Mae."

"I think . . ." Jennifer said, backing up to wrap her little arms around my legs, ". . . no touch her."

Maggie Mae decided it was her job to protect Lori and clearly, didn't want anyone near her. Even though the dog was no bigger than Lori's forearm, the barking and growling prevented me from reaching out to her. Since nearly losing an arm from being mauled by those two dogs seven years earlier, I still had a small fear.

"That's a very loyal little dog you have Lori, but I don't think she likes us."

"She's just protective," Lori said as she kissed Maggie Mae on the top of her head. "I'll put her back in the bathroom. Be right back!"

Lori adored Maggie Mae.

CRESO

After living in a warm climate for fifteen years, acclimating to the frigid humid atmosphere of Michigan proved difficult for me. Working as an outside sales rep meant constantly moving from my warm car or client's office out into blowing, flesh-biting, arctic winds. I ended up in the hospital suffering from pneumonia and pleurisy. The doctor told me if I wanted to live beyond forty years of age, I needed to move to a warmer, drier climate. I was thirty-nine.

After being released from the hospital, I came home and discovered one of my cats was missing, Tabitha. Despite posting signs and visiting the animal shelter numerous times, I never saw her again. My heart ached. Maybe this was a sign I really needed to move on? I knew I had some decisions to make. I needed to talk with Lori.

That Saturday, I bundled up Jennifer in her pink polka dot snowsuit and white rubber boots, then drove us west five miles to Lori's home.

The sun glistened off the snow that had fallen during the night. It looked beautiful, but I slipped a few times on ice patches as I made my way to Lori's side door. Jennifer followed me, while attempting to scoop up snow to make snowballs.

"Who is it?" I heard Lori ask through the door.

"Bonny and Jennifer."

"Oh, just a minute, hon."

I heard Maggie barking, then a door close, and finally, the side door opened revealing Lori.

"I need to talk with you, Lor. Do you have time now?"

"Sure. Steve is at work, and I don't go in until two this afternoon. Come on in," Lori said as she held open the door.

Jennifer was engrossed in her snowball-making attempts. "Honey, come on in." Jennifer looked up at me obviously not happy with my request. "I'm sure you can find something to play with in here." Jennifer reluctantly obeyed.

After setting my daughter up with some paper, pens and crayons in the living room, Lori and I sat down at the kitchen table with our coffee. "What's up?" Lori asked.

I wasn't sure how Lori would react to my news. She knew I'd been in the hospital. She also knew my mother had died from asthma at an age we were now fast approaching.

"Lor, the doctor told me that I will not survive to see age forty if I stay here. I need to do something. Since Jennifer's father is out of the picture, and my dad refuses to help, I'm all she has. I've got to do whatever I can to ensure I'm around for her."

"Of course you do." Lori said as she put her hands over my clasped ones.

"The doctor said I need to move back to a warmer, drier climate."

"So are you returning to Texas?"

"I thought about it, but if I ran into Jennifer's father, I'd melt like a pad of butter in a hot pan. I still love him but the feelings are not reciprocated. I refuse to return there to run the chance of being hurt all over again. So, I know this is going to sound nuts, but I taped up a map of the world on the wall and threw darts . . . to narrow down where I'm going to live. The darts landed on a small island in the Caribbean named St. Maarten; Sydney, Australia and San Diego, California."

"You do live by your motto!"

"No guts, no glory?" I asked.

"Yep. To move to any of those places not knowing anyone, or having any connections or even a job—that's gutsy. I couldn't do it." Lori stood up, "Do you want some more coffee?"

"Sure." I peaked into the living room and saw Jennifer engrossed in drawing something. I turned back toward Lori. "Or crazy. Australia is a little too scary, even for me, and St. Maarten is an island, and I think I'd get bored after awhile, you know how I like to drive and explore, so I've decided on San Diego."

"Have you ever been there before?" Lori asked as she lit a cigarette. The smoke bothered me, but I didn't say anything, as it was her house.

"No. Never. But, I've been checking it out on the Internet, and as soon as I have my house under contract, I'm flying out there to find an apartment. I'll worry about a job once I'm there."

"So, how soon are we talking about you leaving?"

"It depends on how soon my house is sold. I'm meeting with three real estate agents this week." I glanced out the window at the snow-covered scenery. "I hear it's paradise there. Once I'm out there, maybe you'll come visit?"

"Maybe." I knew Lori didn't like traveling. She had never once visited me in either Austin or Monterey. I didn't hold high hopes she'd come to San Diego either.

"So what do you think? Am I nuts?"

"You're not nuts. You're gutsy. You have balls—more balls than most men. You're a cat, you always land on your feet, and I don't think that will change. I think San Diego is a good plan, if that's what you want."

"Thanks, Lor. You've made me feel better. This is scary, but really exciting too." I got up and walked to the sink, rinsed out my coffee cup and placed it upside down on the counter to air dry.

"You know, no matter where I go or what I do, you are always my best friend. I love ya, Lor."

"Right back at ya," Lor said as we embraced.

Lori had to get ready for work, and I needed to start making my plans.

Two short months later, Jennifer and I drove across the country to our new apartment overlooking mountains and Lake Hodges in San Diego, leaving the cold of Michigan, and Lori, behind.

16
LIFE IS GOOD

Shortly after our arrival in San Diego, I located a wonderful pre-school for my daughter and I accepted a position writing newsletter content.

"Too bad you couldn't have moved three months later, then you could have watched Marie graduate," Lori said.

I cradled the phone between my ear and shoulder as I put Jennifer in her booster seat at the dining room table and handed her some crayons and coloring books. "Did she get the gift I sent?"

"Yes, and thanks."

"So what's Marie doing now?"

"She's working at one of the German restaurants in Frankenmuth . . . and she's got a boyfriend!"

"Yeah?"

"We'll see how it goes."

I heard Lori take a drag of her cigarette. "Next June is Ken's graduation. Do you think you'll be able to fly home for it, *Aunt Bonny*?"

"Oh, Lor I hate to make any promises. It depends on what happens here, and if I can afford the plane ticket and the time away from work. So, for now, no promises."

"I understand."

❦

Over the next year, I worked constantly. I felt bad about missing both of my godchildren's high school graduations, but I couldn't afford the time, travel and expense. I mailed Ken a card with a little gift, just as I had to Marie.

Two months later, just after Jennifer's fourth birthday, we moved into our new home: one side of a two-story duplex, constructed of beige adobe and brown wood. The high ceilings and open floor plan were nice, but the bright natural light coming in through the many windows overlooking the spectacular view of the mountains had sold me.

With my time stretched between taking care of Jennifer, working a full-time job and packing, moving and unpacking, I'd not had a chance to call Lori.

I put my daughter down for her afternoon nap upstairs then stepped outdoors. "Hi, Lori. So how's life with both of your babies graduated?"

"It's so different now, Bon."

"I bet." I sat on the large wooden deck in the backyard of my home looking at the vista of mountains as I talked with her while Inky rubbed my leg. "I can't even imagine my life without Jennifer here every day. So how are you and Steve adjusting to the empty nest?"

"Well, Steve works all day long and comes home exhausted about the time I'm leaving to go work nights at *Boysville*. We're like two ships passing through with a polite nod. I'm awfully glad to have my little Maggie Mae here to keep me company during the days."

"Yeah, Inky is right here with me. She's already eleven years old. The men come in and out of my life, but Inky is the one constant. I dread the day I lose her."

"Bon, don't think about that."

"I can't help it, Lor, because . . . did I tell you that we lost Samantha to a coyote on Christmas Eve?"

"On no!"

"Yeah, it was sad; tore my heart apart. It came right up to our back door and pulled her off the carpeted cat tree then ran away with her. By the time I caught up, all that was left was parts of her fur. That's why I'm so glad to have my little Inker Stinker here with me. Yet I worry about her; she's a lot older than Sammy was."

"I'm so sorry."

I reached out to pet Inky. "Thanks."

"On a happier note," Lori said, "I've started baking a lot. The boys at the home love it. I'm always taking cookies over there, especially over the holidays, like Christmas, Easter, Valentine's Day, St. Patrick's Day and the fourth of July."

I easily envisioned Lori working like mad to bake hundreds of cookies, with her kitchen completely covered in flour. I laughed.

"I don't eat many of the cookies," she said, "just give them to the boys, and I've also started visiting my elderly neighbors. A lot of them are homebound, so I think they like me visiting and taking the time to talk with them at least once every other day."

"I'm sure they do."

"Since most don't have relatives nearby, it's my way of checking on them. We just talk and I try to help them in any way I can."

"I don't know many people that take the time to get to know their neighbors anymore, let alone bring them cookies. That's really sweet of you, Lor."

"It's nothing special," she said. "Hey, did I tell you because Steve works so much, we started having "date" days. Every Sunday we do something fun together like driving out in the country or strolling through the parks around here. It's so sweet how he holds my hand when we walk. I really enjoy the walks because we talk about anything and everything that pops into our heads. I actually feel closer to Steve now than I ever have. This week we're going to go check out antique shops. I just hope I don't find too many things I used to play with, because that will make me feel old!"

I smiled. "Well, Lor, I hate to tell you this, but the last time I lived in Saginaw, I went to the antique mall there on Michigan Avenue with Angie and we ran across a Barbie Dream House just like the one I had as a kid." I paused. "Yeah, you're right, it's gonna make you feel old. Just remember you're not! I still feel sixteen on the inside, don't you?"

"Yeah, I do. I wonder when we'll start feeling old? I hope never."

"I don't think we will. I asked my dad once how old he felt, and he said on the inside he still felt young, that's why every time he looked in the mirror it surprised him to see this older guy staring back at him."

We both laughed.

"Did I tell you Steve got me a new digital camera and I've started taking photographs?"

"No. That's a great gift! I just have my old automatic. So what do you take photos of?"

"Maggie, mostly. I take her on walks through the backyard to the school or over to the park. I've gotten some great shots of squirrels and flowers and sunsets, too."

"I'd love to see them, Lori."

"I'll send you some, or better yet, when you come to visit, you can see them all."

"How about you come out here to visit?" I asked Lori once again.

"Bon, you know I won't fly and don't like traveling. You're going to have to come here."

"Yeah, yeah. You know I'm never going to stop asking you to come visit. Lori, you've got to get out of Michigan and see, at a minimum, the USA. It's so awesome here with the mountains and the oceans and all the different plants and trees—even the squirrels are different. You really should try traveling!"

"Nope."

"Okay, I gave it a shot."

"You'll never stop."

"You're right." I said, laughing.

Lori's talent in photography grew with each photo she sent of landscapes, birds, and close-ups of flowers or leaves. The majority of the photos, however, featured Maggie; dressed in costumes for Halloween, Christmas, Easter or Valentine's Day. Lori constantly showered her love over her little fur-baby, Maggie Mae.

Bonny Brookes

17
STORM ARISING

When the time came for my daughter to begin kindergarten, I decided to return to Texas to put her through school. As much as I loved San Diego, I didn't love their school system. I called the real estate broker, who helped me purchase my first home so many years ago, and he offered to be my sponsoring broker if I returned to Austin and got my real estate license. The idea of working with no salary scared yet excited me. I had nothing to lose and it was time to move on.

I was amazed that my house sold just a few hours after I placed an ad online. A few weeks later, I found myself loading my belongings on a U-haul truck, driving my car onto the attached trailer, and playing open-road truck driver on yet another adventure across the country with my daughter and our two remaining cats, Inky and Mr. Bobbit. Jennifer celebrated her fifth birthday as we traveled east on Interstate 10.

"I'm back in Texas, Lor."

"Really? Well, that doesn't surprise me. You always loved it there."

We spent an hour catching up on each other's lives. Ken still lived with his friends and Marie's relationship looked serious. Steve's two kids had also grown up and moved on.

After we hung up, I realized all Lori talked about were the four kids and Maggie. She hadn't shared anything about herself or Steve. I had a feeling something was amiss.

ॐ

I enjoyed great success in real estate and in other areas of my life during my first eighteen months back in Texas.

"Did you hear about the earthquake?" I asked Lori over the phone.

"The one in Seattle yesterday?"

"Yeah. Well, I called to tell you WHY the earth moved!"

Lori laughed. "Okay . . . why?"

"Because after all these years I have finally met a man I'm actually attracted to!"

Lori laughed. "How did you meet?"

"Now, don't laugh, okay?"

"Okay."

"On New Year's Eve I got on the website Love at AOL and went shopping for a man."

"Seriously? Is that like a candy store selling men instead of candy?" Lori said before she burst into giggles.

"Hey, you're laughing. You promised!"

"Sorry," Lori said bringing her laughter under control.

"It's a dating site on the Internet. Anyway, I narrowed the choices down to three guys. Two responded back. I met the first guy over a month ago; no sparks. The other guy—it took nearly two months for us to finally meet. In his picture, he looked like a nice Jewish boy with his glasses and slicked-back brown hair. But, when I walked into the coffee shop, I didn't see anyone resembling that picture. What I did see was a gorgeous guy wearing a denim blue shirt and blue jeans, with long wavy brown hair and a strong square jawline. He looked like Patrick Swayze. Oh my God, he was *gorgeous!*" My enthusiasm bubbled over as I shared my story with Lori. "I stood there thinking, *too bad that isn't the guy I'm meeting!*"

"So that wasn't him?" Lori asked.

"Actually, as I looked around the room one more time to find the nice Jewish man, that gorgeous guy stood up, all five feet eleven inches of him and asked me if I was Bonny. I about died. It *was* him!"

"Really?"

"Yeah. We ended up talking for an hour at the coffee shop until I had to pick up my daughter from daycare. He followed me and then treated all of us to dinner at a Mexican restaurant. Lori, I feel like I've met my soulmate. He says he likes everything I do, like water skiing, traveling, music, animals and . . . my daughter adores him. She sat in his lap after dinner, combed his hair with her fingers, hugged him around the neck, and he had the biggest smile on his face. To top it off, he even puts up with my cats. I feel so lucky!"

"Wow, Bon . . . that is great! See, I told you you'd meet 'the one' someday. Your day is here."

"I hope so. Every time I think about him, a rush goes flying through my stomach. I feel like a teenager in love. It's been so long! I didn't realize how empty my life was until I met him. Suddenly I feel alive again."

"So does he have a name?" Lori asked.

"Keith."

Lori began the familiar childhood poem, "Keith and Bonny sitting in a tree, K-I-S-S-I-N-G."

"Very funny, Lor."

"I'm teasing you. So have you met his family?"

"No. He's from New York, the Bronx. He told me he left home at seventeen. His mother and two brothers are still there and his father is dead."

"Doesn't sound like he has close family ties."

"No, except with his stepmother, who lives in Florida."

"Well, at least that's one person. You know how important I think family is. It's the foundation for our lives."

"You're blessed to have a nice big family, Lor. In many ways Keith and I are alike, in that I also left home early, one of my parents is dead, and I don't have close family ties either. So I think we're good together and for each other."

"I'm so happy for you. I can't wait to meet him. Send me photos, okay?"

"Let's see if this lasts, first. If he sees me more than two times, I promise I'll take a photo and mail it to you."

"I'm so happy for you, Bon. Hey, speaking of love, Marie is getting married this summer to that guy she's been dating for years. Do you think you can make it? The wedding will be in Frankenmuth."

"Lori, that's so exciting! I will really, really try. I'll let you know for sure later. Do you like Marie's fiancé?"

"Yes, both Steve and I do. Marie is so happy and that's really what matters."

"You're right."

Once again I realized after we hung up, Lori had never mentioned how things with her and Steve were going. Once again, she'd only spoken of the four kids and her dog.

⚜

Keith and I saw each other every day. Our kids, his teen-aged son, Michael, and my daughter, loved being around each other and even our pets, his dog and cat and my cats got along.

After two months of being together, we all went to Houston to visit my grandmother. She had never liked any of my boyfriends, so I didn't have much hope she'd like Keith either.

After a several-hour visit, Keith left to pull his pick-up truck up to the entry, while Jennifer and I waited outside with Grandmother. "So what do you think of him?"

Grandmother looked at me, took my hand in hers and said, "Honey, he's one in a million, if you don't marry him, I will."

Her response stunned me. "Really?"

She smiled. "Really."

☙❧

"Hey Lor, how are you doing?"

"Bonny! I'm fine. What's up with you?"

"Well, you'd better sit down."

"Oh no."

I laughed. "No, Lor, it's good news. At least, I think so."

"Yeah? Spill."

"Though it wasn't after a wonderful dinner in a dimly-lit fancy restaurant with champagne, Keith asked me to marry him."

"That's fantastic!" I heard her light up a cigarette. "Tell me how he did it."

"Very casually. We were at his house. The kids were playing in the backyard and he asked me to come see something in his bedroom."

"Ooh-la-la"

"No, Lori. Nothing like that. I sat on the bed and he grabbed a box off his dresser and tossed it over to me and said, 'I want you to have that.'"

"Was it a diamond ring?"

"Not exactly. It was his father's turquoise ring that had some itty-bitty diamond chips."

"Well, turquoise is your birthstone."

"Good memory, Lor!"

"Did he say anything else?"

"Yeah, he said because the kids and pets got along so well, and I needed health insurance and he needed a wife; he thought we should get hitched."

"Like that?"

"Yep. Not exactly romantic."

"So . . . ?"

"I said okay, since I think this will be my only chance to get married, and Jennifer really needs a father figure."

"Do you love him?"

"Thinking about him makes my stomach do somersaults and I do enjoy being with him and being taken care of for once in my life, so yes, I love him."

"Have you set a date?"

"We're thinking in August on what would-have-been my mother's birthday. That's six weeks after Marie's wedding. I'm hoping we can rent a paddlewheel boat to travel around Lake Travis and have the ceremony and reception on it. Will you be able to come?"

"Oh, Bon, I'm not sure. I'll talk to Steve, but you know how I am about traveling. Are you coming to Marie's wedding?"

"Yes."

"Well, if I can't come to your wedding, I'll see you at Marie's and give you our gift then. Okay?"

I was disappointed. "I sure wish you'd take a chance and travel, Lori. But, if you don't come, I'll just have to get over it, won't I?"

"I'm sorry, Bonny. I really am. I love you."

"Love you, too."

"So how are you and Steve doing?" I asked.

"Same old stuff. We both work all the time and with Marie's wedding coming up," Lori chuckled, "it's really better if he stays out of my way."

I knew how Lori was when she had a mission, and she was right. I hoped they were getting along, but I still wondered.

18
WEDDING BELLS

The phone rang early one morning. It had to be Lori, she never could remember that I was an hour behind her. "You are coming for Marie's wedding, right?"

"Yes! We're all coming."

"You're bringing your fiancé?"

Just a few days earlier, Keith and I had gone to the JP to get married. Since this was my first marriage, I had wanted to have a real wedding. Keith didn't care; it was his second marriage and he couldn't help pay for the paddlewheel boat or the ceremony or the reception. If I wanted the wedding of my dreams, I needed to foot the entire bill. I planned to do just that until I learned none of my family was willing to make the trip to Austin. That hurt me deeply and Keith saw that and took the opportunity to convince me to just go to the Justice of the Peace. I was incredibly disappointed and felt I'd been cheated out of what most brides experienced; but in the end, I agreed. Nobody in my family, or even Lori, knew I had gotten married. We figured after Marie's wedding, we'd make the announcement to my family and friends. "Ah, yeah, and Michael and Jennifer."

"Oh that's wonderful! I really can't wait to meet your new love . . . and see sweet little Jennifer again." Lori paused. "Hey, listen, Hon, I've got a gazillion things to do. I'll see you soon, and get here safely. Love ya."

For the first time since I was a kid, someone else did the driving on a cross-country trip. Keith drove quietly, except when we crossed the state lines; then he suddenly came to life honking the horn and whooping with excitement. Michael and Jennifer sat in the small back seat of the pickup truck teasing each other constantly while I enjoyed the scenery of Texas, Arkansas, Tennessee, Kentucky, Indiana and Michigan along the way. After three days in the truck, the kids were glad to escape their small quarters. Another first was checking into a motel, rather than staying with my father. With four of us, it didn't seem right to impose.

"Lor, we're here!" I announced over our motel room's phone. We had just unpacked, and the kids had gone to see the swimming pool.

"Oh, Bon! I'm so glad you made it. I don't have time to see you until the wedding, though. Do you know how to get there?" Lori asked.

"I completely understand *Mother-of-the-Bride*. We'll find our way. We're going to visit my dad and Andrew today, but I can't wait to see you at the wedding, Lori!"

"Me neither. Love you!"

"Love you too. See ya soon."

I hung up and looked at Keith over my shoulder, "It's time to go visit my dad and tell him the news. Let's get the kids and go."

We drove the short distance to Father's home. Angie answered the door and let us in. After introductions, we went into the dining room, where my father was sitting at the head of the table, with a white walking stick in his hand.

I went over and hugged him then Jennifer did the same.

"Is that my little princess?" Father asked as he put his arm around Jennifer who was trying to climb into his lap. Father dropped his white cane to help Jennifer reach her goal.

After they were both settled, I introduced Keith and Michael.

"Dad . . . what's with the cane?"

"Oh, where is my cane?" Father asked using his foot to feel around to find it. Keith reached down and picked it up, then put it in Father's hand.

Father folded it up and then reopened it. "Isn't that nice?" he said.

"Yeah, nice . . . but, Dad, why do you have a cane and why are you wearing dark glasses inside the house?"

"Oh, I guess I didn't tell you."

"Tell me what?"

He went on to explain that he had developed cataracts and due to his diabetes, macular degeneration was beginning to occur.

"The eye doctor thought by removing the cataract, my sight would be greatly improved so I could continue reading and driving and doing my puzzles. So, I had laser surgery." Father said then stopped like that was the whole story.

I grew very concerned something had gone terribly wrong. "And?"

"Well, the doctor botched it."

"Botched it? Where did you go?"

"Detroit, to the college."

"You let some *students* mess with your eyes?"

"It was a lot cheaper."

"You are always the cheap Scotsman, Dad, but when it comes to your health, going to the lowest-cost doctor is not a good idea. What happened?"

"Well, the doctor, I guess . . . ," Father swallowed then continued, "something about his fingernail touched the laser instrument, which made it move, where it shouldn't have," he explained as if talking about damage to someone else's eye, "which severed the optic nerve."

I shot up off my seat, "Severed your optic nerve?"

"Now calm down, Bonny."

"Dad, it's your eyes. Can it be repaired?"

"No," Father said solemnly.

"So what, you're completely blind now?"

"Not completely, the other eye I can see colors and shadows and outlines of objects, it's just the details I can't see."

I pressed on. "So you're telling me you are completely blind in the one eye with no hope of ever regaining your sight?"

"Yes."

"Sue the doctor!"

"No, I'm not going to raise a stink. Plus I signed release papers before they did the procedure saying I couldn't sue."

"*Dad*! Forget the papers, sue the doctor!"

"No." There was Father's disciplinary voice. "Let it go, Bonny, I mean it." He would not listen to me. I was fuming and angry, but I knew better than to press any further with my father. I looked at Angie. She smiled at me shaking her head, as if to say she'd tried to get him to do the same thing, with the same result I'd just experienced. I had no choice but to let it go.

"Changing the subject, Dad, Keith and I got married."

"You got married? I thought you planned to rent a boat in August. We were going to work on some arrangements to come down."

Completely taken aback, I said, "You were? Had I known, Dad . . . yes, that's what I wanted to do, but when you said you couldn't make it, I figured what's the point of having a wedding when my dad won't even be there to give me away?"

"I suppose."

I began to wonder if it had something to do with his eyes. At this point, I didn't dare ask. He'd already made it clear it was not a subject he wanted to talk about. Once again, I felt like the little girl who only wanted her father's blessing and approval, and yet once again had been cut to the core by his lack of openness and support.

As always, I hid the hurt and pain by acting as if all was well. "We need to run," I said.

"Oh? Where are you going next?"

"Over to introduce Andrew to everyone."

"Let me get this straight, you're taking your husband to meet your old boyfriend?"

Father never understood why I maintained friendships. To me, friends are to be cherished because they made life fuller. Good friends, who fully knew and appreciated me, were hard to come by. I cherished my friends, no matter how our friendship started. "Yes."

"Bonny, when you break up with someone, you are to cut all ties. You shouldn't even be talking to Andrew anymore. My God, you broke his heart over twenty years ago."

"Dad, you just don't understand. Andrew and I are friends. We're more like a very close brother and sister. There are no romantic feelings between us and there haven't been in two decades. Haven't you ever been good friends with someone of the opposite sex?"

"No. It's not possible."

"Well, Andrew and I are living proof it *is* possible."

My father was getting my goat, again. He wouldn't listen; he would never see someone else's point of view. I didn't want to deal with it any longer.

"We've got to go now." I said reaching to pull Jennifer off her grandfather's lap.

Father rose to walk us to the door. "Okay, thanks for stopping by."

Andrew, as always, was welcoming and truly happy to hear our news. He and my husband seemed to hit it off right away. I was relieved. I had really wanted Andrew to like Keith.

The next morning we woke up early to prepare for Marie's wedding. The sun shone brightly, not a cloud in the sky, and the air was warm but not humid. It was a perfect day for a beautiful wedding between my goddaughter and her soon-to-be husband.

The wedding took place in an old-fashioned fieldstone church in a small mid-Michigan German town. Steve proudly walked Marie down the aisle to her awaiting groom. She wore her blonde hair in a bun atop her head elongating her porcelain colored neck. She looked so grown up—so different from that little girl sitting on her bed looking up at me with big blue eyes so many years ago. Little Marie had grown up and gotten married. Where had the years gone?

She floated around the reception in her full-length white satin wedding gown as she danced with her husband, her stepfather, her brother and her uncles.

Since we were young, Lori always dressed casually in jeans or shorts, but today she looked more beautiful than I'd ever seen her. She wore a beautiful white A-Line dress covered by a white sheer overlay decorated with deep rose pink flowers. The corsage, pinned near her left shoulder, matched the outfit perfectly. Happiness radiated across her face. Even her posture had changed. She stood more erect as she strutted around the reception like a peacock while her husband sat at the family's table.

CRSD

Two days after the wedding, I took Father over to Lori's house, leaving my husband in charge of our kids. I needed to break the news of my marriage to her. I sincerely hoped she wouldn't be hurt by the secret I'd kept from her.

I called through the screen door at the side of the house,

"Hi, Lor!"

"Bonny? Is that you?"

"Yep, and Dad."

"Come on in, hon!"

I held Father's elbow to help guide him into Lori's small home and get him comfortably seated at the kitchen table.

"Welcome to my home, Mr. Brookes."

"Hello Lori. It's been a long time since I've seen you," my father said. I knew he was using the verb *see* out of habit, but the irony of it hit me. I couldn't help but smile.

"It has been." Lori gave me a quick squeeze before I sat down next to Father. "Would you like a cup of coffee?" she asked.

My father and I responded in unison, "Yes!"

"Marie's wedding was perfect, Lor. You did good, kid," I said smiling at her. She smiled back. "Hey, I've been keeping a secret I need to let you in on, Lor."

"Yeah?"

I took a sip of the coffee she handed to me. "You know how Keith and I planned on getting married in August and renting the boat and everything?" I asked.

"Yeah, I'm really sorry we can't come down for that, Bon. Really."

"So am I, but you weren't the only one, Lor. Dad here told me he and Angie couldn't make it, so to cut to the chase, Keith and I went to the JP last month and got hitched. It took a whopping four minutes, and then after eating breakfast at Denny's, Keith went to work for the day. I couldn't believe that he would go to work rather than spend our—I gestured air quotes—*wedding day* together. Lor, maybe it's me; maybe I expected too much, but that was a huge letdown, not the way I envisioned how my wedding day would be, but it's done and I'm married. I didn't tell you sooner, because I didn't want to rain on Marie's parade."

"Oh, Bon!" Lori said getting up to give me a hug. "See, I told you you'd get married someday. I'm sorry the wedding wasn't what you wanted, but it's the marriage that matters."

"Speaking of marriages, how are you and Steve doing? You bounced all over the place at Marie's wedding, but Steve stayed sitting at the table, it seemed, for almost the entire event."

"He doesn't like crowds or socializing. I do. He's fine."

I wasn't really asking about how Steve was doing, but how *they* were getting along. I figured Lori didn't want to talk about it in front of my father, so I let it drop.

"How are you doing, Mr. Brookes?" Lori asked him. He started telling her all about his eyes, doctor visits, his daily morning coffee hours with his male friends at the donut shop and he droned on and on. It made me think Father, not being able to work anymore, was lonely at home.

Lori was so gracious and sweet and concerned about him. I focused on dealing with his needs in the moment: helping him in and out of the car, through the door, to his seat, and now putting the coffee cup in his hand as I saw Father reaching out trying to find it.

I looked up and caught Lori watching me. A tear slipped down her cheek.

"Lori, are you okay?" I asked suddenly concerned.

"Yes, I'm fine," she said as she motioned me to follow her into the other room.

I nodded then turned toward my father, "Dad, we'll be right back."

"Okay," he said as he fumbled with the spoon in his coffee cup.

"Lor, why are you crying?"

Lori pulled me into a hug and stroked my hair. I had been so wrapped up in helping my father that I didn't understand Lori's tears.

"Bon, you have always been so strong . . . and here you are, still so strong, going through this."

I was clueless about what had Lori so upset. "What?"

"Your dad."

Then it hit me, really hit me. My father's age; his sudden blindness. He would never see what my husband looked like; he would never see Jennifer except as a little girl.

"Lor, there's a time for this, and right now, I can't do it." My natural defense of blocking pain by ignoring it was back in play. "Okay?"

Lori hugged me again. "Okay, just know I'm always here for you, Bon. If your dad needs help, call me, we'll take him wherever he needs to go, or if he needs meals, or whatever. Promise me."

"Thanks, Lori. I promise."

Over the next three years, I did ask Lori and Steve to check on Father. Although he could no longer work, his wife did, so Father spent most of his time home alone. Lori and Steve went to work as protective angels in my father's life.

Bonny Brookes

19
MEN

Upon arrival back in Texas, and after unpacking, I realized Lori and I had spent a great deal of time together, but we never really had a chance to talk about her. We talked about others, the care of others, the lives of others, but not about her. I had a nugget deep in my gut that something was wrong. Knowing Lori, she didn't tell me because she didn't want to burden me. I decided to press her on it the next time we spoke.

I began calling my father every other week. With each call, his voice sounded weaker and sadder. He told me since he could no longer work, watch TV, read or put together his beloved jigsaw puzzles; he had nowhere to go or people to talk to, so he just sat around with his cat, Charlie, on his lap.

Concerned, I called Lori and asked her opinion. She and Steve visited with him each week and she said he seemed fine.

"He's always joking or sharing some trivial political or historical story with us." I felt somewhat reassured. Father loved that stuff and knew lots about it. But as time passed, he felt increasingly worthless and helpless. Emotionally, he slipped down a dark hole of unhappiness. He became depressed and I grew concerned he may even turn suicidal. Angie, as sole-breadwinner, had taken a better-paying job—in Detroit. That left Father alone during the week to fend for himself. Accidents like tripping down the stairs and burning his hand on the stovetop while cooking, happened frequently.

At his wife's and doctor's pleading, Father enrolled in a program for the blind designed to teach him how to cope and care for himself. He stayed in a dormitory at the school, while he learned how to dress himself, cook, take public transportation and learn new hobbies, like making doormats.

Four weeks into the program, the school announced it was closing for maintenance over the weekend and all students would need to go home. Because his wife worked two hours away, she couldn't pick up Father. He would need to use the skills he had learned to take a bus from Lansing to Saginaw, a ninety-mile trip.

I called to make sure Father got home safely that night. He sounded stronger than he had the last time I spoke to him, but he sat in that big house all alone and said he couldn't find his cat. When I called a few days later, he told me the cat had been euthanized shortly after he left for school. Father hadn't been pre-informed and was devastated. Charlie had been his loyal companion.

Father grew more and more depressed after that. He started sounding like an old man, despite only being in his early seventies. My concern mounted and I called Lori frequently.

Eventually Father decided his wife didn't want him and he was only a burden to her. He wanted to live with someone who was around all the time. When I offered to bring him to live with us, he refused, claiming it was too hot in Texas. I didn't argue the matter, since it really wasn't a convenient time to bring someone else into our house. Life was stressful enough with Keith and I working full-time, raising two kids and caring for the pets, so I knew I wouldn't be able to devote the time necessary for my father's needs.

I suggested he might consider living with his recently-widowed older sister—in Florida. He said he didn't want to live there either. I called my Aunt Martha anyway and ran the idea past her, which she loved. After several months of considering different options, Father finally agreed to stay with her. I called Lori to let her know that.

"Lori, we're heading up to Michigan to move Dad to Florida."

"Oh, Bonny, I'll be happy to see you, but I really love your dad too, and I'll miss him. When will you be here?"

"In about two days."

"Okay, I'll see ya soon."

We hung up. No small talk. No talking about Lori. I still had that feeling in my gut that Lori wasn't sharing something. But then, I wasn't sharing my troubles about Keith either. I guess there were some things we didn't want to talk about, because it'd make them seem more real.

The trip this time had been silent. Keith's son did not join us. Jennifer's favorite cat, Mr. Bobbit, had died shortly before we left. He had choked to death on one of her toy beads. My little baby felt guilty and sad about her kitty's death. There was no laughing, joking or teasing on this trip. Simply silence. When we arrived at my father's place two days later, Lori and Steve joined us within minutes. After three years of taking care of him, they loved him as much as if he were their own father.

Because of Keith's work schedule, we only had twenty-four hours in town to pack up Father's belongings before starting the trip to Florida and then we would have to leave there immediately to get back to Texas. At least with Father riding with us on part of the journey, it was more enjoyable. Otherwise, the long, deathly-silent trip was miserable.

As Steve and my husband assisted my father, I pulled Lori aside. "Lori, I really want some time with just us girls so we can talk, really talk."

Lori looked me in the eyes, "What do you want to talk about?"

"You. Me. Our lives. Our men. Are you happy? That kind of stuff."

"I'm fine," Lori said as usual. "But, I'm happy to talk. We can go over to my house."

I walked over to the men and asked no one in particular, "Lori and I need a little 'girl time.' Would you mind if I took Jennifer and we went over to the house for about an hour?"

My father, looking off to the side, not knowing exactly where I stood, said, "You go. The guys and I are fine." Steve and Keith nodded.

So Lori, Jennifer and I headed over to her place. Maggie greeted us, barking as ferociously as ever.

"I'll put her in the bathroom, so she doesn't bite you."

"That'd be great," I replied. "Maggie's just never liked us!"

Once we were safely in the house, Jennifer went into the living room and watched TV. Lori and I sat at the table in the kitchen and, as always, drank coffee while talking.

"Lor, I'm worried about you . . . well, not worried, but I just have this concern that all is not as it seems, like there's something you're not telling me. Should I be worried?"

"I'm fine," Lori said as she lit a cigarette, avoiding my eyes.

I didn't believe her. "Really?"

"Yeah."

"How is life with both Ken and Marie gone? How are you and Steve?"

"You know Ken had moved into an apartment with a few other guys."

"Yeah. How's he doing? Does he like it?"

Lori laughed as she got up to open the door off the kitchen to Ken's room. "I guess he didn't; he's back home!"

"Really?" I peeked in and saw his belongings thrown in haphazardly. "Well, the real world is a lot harder now than back when we were—" I stopped. I had forgotten for a brief moment how Lori had suffered.

She let it slide and closed the door. "Yeah, it is. Actually, I'm glad to have Ken home. I really missed him."

"How is married life treating you, Bon?"

"Honestly?"

"Uh-oh. Something wrong?" Lori knew me too well.

"Well, let's just say it's not what I thought being married would be like."

"Spill."

"I'll spill if you spill."

Lori sat quiet for a moment looking at her fingers, then looked up. "Okay, deal."

"Well, our 'honeymoon' was a complete joke. Keith had to go to France on business. He told me to buy my own ticket if I wanted to join him. He ended up working most of the time, and expected me to do his laundry and go find things to do to fill up the days I spent alone. One day I went into town wearing a knapsack, filled with dirty laundry, on my back and got lost while looking for a laundromat. It was very scary, not knowing where I was and not being able to communicate with anyone. Thankfully, I finally found my way back to the car, but I didn't get his clothes washed. When I picked him up from work, I was still freaking out. All he did was berate me for being late. He didn't care. And that's the highlight."

"Oh, Bon, that's terrible. How long had you been married at that point?"

"Three months. He works all the time, most of it in Malaysia or Taiwan. He doesn't have to travel, he volunteers to go, like he's single with no responsibilities. Did I tell you about the day we got married, that four-minute ceremony where the JP forgot what she was saying in the middle?"

Lori nodded.

"If that's not an omen, I don't know what is! How many men do you know who just got married prefer to go to work, rather than spend that day with their new wife? That's what Keith did!"

"Yeah, you told me."

"That's not all. He often uses his work as an excuse why he can't be at big events, like school functions for the kids, holidays, etcetera. Yes, he travels a good portion of the time, and I understand he's tired, but he volunteers for it. He seems to forget I work a lot of hours as well; but, that doesn't count. He expects me to take care of everything at home, and when he's home, to be there for him and sit with him while he's watching TV or drinking beer."

"Oh, Bon."

"Maybe I expect too much; I don't know. To me, a happy marriage is what I saw between my parents and between my grandparents. Sure, they argued, but they loved each other and wanted to be with each other. I think Keith married me for my money to get his butt out of debt and to be a mother to his son, that's it. When he's home, all he wants to do is stare at the TV or drink beer. He never wants to go out or get together with friends. He doesn't want to have any kids. In the beginning, I really thought I'd love to have another baby. But, nope that's not going to happen. He told me he's fixed. Probably for the best anyway."

"I'm sorry, Bon . . ."

"He also doesn't want me working—maybe because I earn more than him. I don't know. Anyway, I'm slowly letting my business go. I like having more free time, but I don't like the fact I'm giving it up for him, not for me."

I got up and filled my coffee cup then turned back to Lori. "But, the biggest issue I have with him are the lies he tells. He'll lie about the simplest things like taking out the trash, to some major stuff."

"Oh, Bon, most guys lie. They say stuff they think we want to hear. They do it to make us feel better."

"Well, that's one way to look at it. But they'll get caught in the end." I sat down at the table. "Remember in the beginning when he told me he loved to water-ski and loved music and loved traveling?" Lori nodded. "Well, they were all lies. He didn't know how to water-ski, he hates traveling and makes me go in the garage to listen to music!"

I leaned back to look around the corner into the living room. Jennifer was engrossed in the TV, so I continued, "Anyway, he didn't even know how to drive my ski boat and crashed it into the dock. He doesn't sing or play an instrument, and he's a horrible traveler."

I glanced at Lori. "I know you don't like to travel, Lor, but at least you're honest about it. Keith said he loved traveling, but on the way to France, all he did was complain rather than sit back and enjoy the experience. Then I drank some champagne, I mean this *was* our honeymoon trip, and he refused to kiss me—because he hates the smell. He's not fun, Lori," I summarized while fishing for a cigarette in my purse. I pulled one out and lit up. "Oh, and yeah, stress . . . I started smoking again."

Lori sat in silence looking at me then lit up a cigarette. "Bon, we all go through ups and downs. Marriage is a compromise. Give and take," she said before looking away.

"Lor, why did you just look away? What's going on with you and Steve? Are you happy?"

Lori looked back at me, as if contemplating if she wanted to say anything. Finally she spoke.

"I can relate to a lot of what you've just said. I'm so lonely, Bon. Steve works all the time, and when he's home, he either watches TV or sleeps. He never wants to talk or spend time with me. I am so lonely." Lori looked down at her cigarette as she rolled it around in the ashtray.

"Man, I wish we lived closer. Phone calls are okay, but being here with you, and talking and supporting each other, I miss it and I miss you, Lor. Why don't you guys move to Texas?"

"My family is here. I wish we could be closer, too. Thank God I have Maggie. I'd go nuts without her."

"Lor, have you told Steve how you feel?"

"I've tried. I don't think he hears me."

"Do you want to get a divorce?"

"I've thought about it, but he's so good to the kids—he is their dad in every sense of the word, and I'm so scared I'd wind up back on welfare. I just can't do it."

"Have you thought about counseling?"

"No, I don't want that. It's okay, though, really. I have Maggie, my garden and photography. It's a lot of fun. Let me show you some pictures."

We got up and went into Marie's old bedroom and, for the next half hour, looked at Lori's photographs. They were good. Very good. She really did have a talent.

Our time together passed quickly. We had to get back to my father and the men we'd just bashed for the past hour.

20
FAMILIES

Delicious aromas filled the house making my mouth water, but it would be at least another hour before we could eat. "Hey Lor, just calling to wish you a Happy Thanksgiving. What are your plans today?"

"Hi! Oh the usual, cooking like crazy with a houseload of family."

"You love it."

"Yeah, you're right. I love all holidays and family get-togethers." I heard some pots clanging, then Lori said, "What are your plans?"

"Nothing much. Keith is cooking and I'm catching up on paperwork. No visitors."

"Well, that's nice that Keith is doing all the cooking—I know that's not your thing."

I laughed. "You're so right! You know me way too well." I stepped outside into the backyard for some privacy before asking, "Hey, Lor. I have an idea for a Christmas gift for Keith I wanted to run past you. I don't know if I'm stepping out of line or not." I heard dishes clattering. *Lori must be setting the table,* I thought.

"What is it?" Lori asked.

"I'm thinking about flying Keith's mother in for Christmas. He left home at seventeen and has not seen her since. I'm going to have to call his stepmother for her contact information, but I think it's important for him to see her again. Do you think I'm sticking my nose in where it doesn't belong?"

The background noise on her end stopped and Lori was silent for a moment. "Well, Bon, I really don't know how things are with his family, but in general, I think that's a great idea. I bet he'll be surprised!"

"That's the plan."

"Well, listen, kiddo, I've got to get back to cooking. Have a great Thanksgiving!"

"You, too."

CRGO

A few days after Thanksgiving, I called Keith's stepmother.

"I wouldn't do that," she advised me.

I thought my idea would be well received. "Why not?"

"You need to talk to Keith."

"I don't understand. What's so bad about being reunited with your parent?"

"You need to talk to Keith."

"You clearly know something I don't. Why won't you tell me?"

"I can't. You need to talk to Keith."

"Okay," I said. Obviously, there was something big Keith had hidden from me, despite my continual questioning him about his family.

I immediately called Lori to share what I'd learned. "He's been lying to me about something else now. It seems everyone else knows what it is, yet me, the wife, I'm left in the dark. I'm ticked."

"Bon, like his stepmother said, you're going to have to talk to your husband."

During dinner that evening, I said, "I thought I'd buy your mother a plane ticket to visit us over Christmas, but your step—"

Keith threw down his fork and jerked up from his seat. "*Hell* no! Don't you dare!"

"What? Why not? I don't understand what the big deal is."

"I don't want that bitch anywhere near me. I left her at seventeen and don't care if I ever see her again."

His explosive reaction frightened me, yet I hid my fear by continuing in a calm, steady tone, "Keith, she's your mom. Whatever she did, you need to forgive her. It's not good to carry grudges. It sucks away your energy. Who knows, this may be the opportunity to mend fences. It could make your life richer . . . and your son's. He's never even met his grandmother, has he?"

"No, and he *never* will. I will *not* have that bitch in my house."

"Okay," I said to Keith's back as he stormed out to his truck and drove away, leaving his dinner on the table.

After cleaning up the uneaten meal, I called Lori and told her what happened.

"Well, I guess it's better to know now rather than having her there and this happening. Be thankful."

"I suppose. I just really wonder why he hates her so much."

"Someday he may tell you, or he may not. You can't worry about it. Let it go."

"Thanks, Lor. I don't know what I'd do without you and your guidance." I grabbed a beer out of the refrigerator and walked out onto the back deck. "So how's your life?"

"Thanksgiving was great. The typical fights and arguments between the kids; good food; and sleeping men in front of football games on the TV." Lori laughed. "I loved it."

"I'm glad to hear that Lori."

"So how are you and Steve doing?" Lori suddenly went silent. The last I knew she felt lonely and wasn't too happy. I wondered if they'd worked things out. "Lor?"

"Yeah, I'm here. We're okay." Her words didn't ring true. "Bon, I'm sorry but I've got to run. We'll talk soon. Love ya," and then she hung up.

I had a nagging feeling something was wrong in her world as well.

Four months later, Keith called me from his office and told me his mother had died.

"Your stepmom?"

"No, my mom."

"So . . . what do you care?"

"What do I care? She's my mom! I need to go to New York."

"Why?"

"To go to the funeral."

"*What*? Wait a minute. You hated the woman. You had a chance to see her over Christmas, but you refused. Now you want to go to her funeral? Why? To make you feel less guilty? What kind of a hypocrite are you?"

"I am going, and as my wife, you should come with me." Obviously, he hadn't listened to a word I had just said.

"There's no way I'm going to go."

"Why not?"

"I've never met the woman. When I offered to have her come visit us, you went ballistic. No, I'm not going to a funeral for a woman I never met and you despised."

"Well, I'm going."

"Do as you want. I don't care."

He left the next day and was gone a week. He called daily telling me how much he loved me and how right I had been about the importance of family. He regretted not allowing me to fly his mother over for the Christmas holidays.

The day before he flew back home, he dropped a bomb when he told me obtained a new credit card and put the entire tab for the funeral on it. Good grief! I no longer understood my husband. I had had it. In fact, I didn't care what he said or did anymore.

The kids were visiting friends and I was in my home office when I heard Keith arrive from the airport. I didn't bother to get up to greet him. I heard him open the refrigerator and then walk back out the front door. *Good*, I thought. I had nothing to say to him anyway.

Thirty minutes later, he came into the house, half-drunk, looking for me. "I'm ready to talk now."

"I think you said all you needed to say on the phone while you were gone."

"I need to fess up to you now."

"About what? Have you told me more lies or hidden more truths?"

"Let's talk outside."

Against my better judgment, I followed Keith to the front door where he had left his suitcase. In our semi-circle driveway, he had set up two chairs separated by a case of beer. Several empty cans rested on their sides under one of the chairs.

"No, I don't want to sit in the driveway in front of all the neighbors. They're all going to think you're a drunk."

"Just come outside. It won't take long."

Reluctantly, I joined him in the driveway. He handed me two packets of photographs from his trip and then cracked opened yet another beer.

I glanced through photographs of men and women I didn't recognize, except for Keith. I put the photographs back in the envelopes and handed them to him. "Who are these people?"

"My family." Keith went on to explain he had several younger brothers and sisters he hadn't told me about. His mother, a drug-abusing prostitute, had been with many men in her life. The people in the photographs were the result of those unions—his siblings; his family. "I want to reconnect with them. Get to know them. Be a part of their lives. I want you to be a part of it as well."

I stared at him, unable to utter a word. He had known about them yet had not told me. Why? "I have asked you on several occasions, point blank, about your family, your parents, your siblings, and now you're telling me you've lied about it all from the get-go?"

"I didn't lie, I just didn't tell you everything."

"You lied by omission. Why?"

"Because you wouldn't have married me."

There was nothing I could say. Our entire marriage had been a farce. Should I let this go and be miserable for the rest of my life married to this man or should I say what's in my heart? I made my decision. "I will tell you, a relationship is based on honesty, trust and respect. You have proven to me, beyond a shadow of a doubt, that I can *not* trust you. At this point, I've lost all respect for you. Obviously you never had enough respect for me to be honest." I walked back into the house, grabbed my cell phone, then got in my convertible car and drove to a nearby park.

"Hey, Lor," I said trying to hide the pain I felt, but I couldn't fool her.

"Bon? Bonny, what's wrong?"

"Oh, Lor . . . my marriage has fallen apart," I said in tears. For the next hour Lori listened as I shared my sorry tale.

"So what are you going to do?" Lori asked.

"I don't know. We've only been married two and half years and stopped sleeping together months ago." I sighed and swiped tears off my cheek. "I don't love him. I don't even like him. I'll never trust him again. I'm such a failure! My dad was right, I *do* have a knack for picking assholes."

"Listen, remember when we were young and formed our ideas about marriage based on our parents' relationships?"

"Yeah."

"Well, think about Jennifer. She's watching the relationship between you and Keith. Is she seeing a happy, supportive and loving marriage?"

"Well, Lor, when you put it like that, no."

"Then there's your answer. You know what to do."

"Thanks, Lor. Thanks for listening. I love ya."

"Love you, too. Hang in there."

I drove home and started making plans.

The year just got worse and worse. Jennifer's godmother, Ann, died from cancer. That same week, the tenants destroyed my rental property that took weeks to repair and re-let. A few days later, the judge signed the divorce decree and Keith moved out—leaving his cat, Tabby, behind.

Keith moved on very quickly. He wed a woman from Malaysia and started a new family. Obviously, he must have had his vasectomy reversed. Just another lie: he did want kids—just not with me.

I called my father hoping he would make me feel better. But he was wrapped up in his own agony. His divorce had just been finalized as well, and now they were trying to sell their beautiful home. He was still angry at the world for his blindness, but continued to refuse to sue the doctors. I tried to encourage him by focusing on the good things, but he wanted none of that. He wanted to feel sorry himself and lashed out at me for wanting to look at things in a new way. I didn't have the strength to deal with it, and made some excuse and got off the phone.

I wanted to go somewhere to think through things. These past few months I'd felt like I was underwater not knowing which way to surface to get air. Once again, I was a single mother with no clear path of where I was going. I had let my business go and now I needed to focus on the basics to ensure we would survive.

I called Lori on several occasions. I really needed her insight, understanding and ideas.

However, Lori's life took on a dimension completely foreign to me. Our conversations revolved around Lori's growing family. Her daughter, Marie, had now given birth to two children: Hunter and Aiden. Lori became a doting grandmother whose life revolved around giving birthday parties, holiday parties and making the mundane seem extraordinary for the young children in her life. She told me all about her preparations and then the expressions on the kids' faces.

I couldn't even begin to wrap my mind around it. My daughter had just celebrated her tenth birthday.

I did realize, once again, Lori never mentioned her husband or their relationship. She focused on the good and happy things in her life. I didn't think it would be right to burden Lori with my woes, so I kept silent.

21
REUNIONS

Two years passed. My conversations with Lori during that time were short. She seemed to always be heading out the door to do things with the kids or grandkids every time I called. I envied her. Her life seemed so full of love and people. Mine seemed so devoid of both—except for Jennifer and our cats. I missed my friend. I missed our heart-to-heart talks.

Jennifer and I drove back "home" for my thirtieth high school reunion. We stayed at the home of my high school boyfriend, Andrew. I hadn't seen him since introducing him to my, now, ex-husband. Andrew had lost most of his blond hair, and had developed a smoker's gravelly voice and cough, but otherwise, he was still the same. We picked up where we had left off. He still had not married and agreed to be my "date" for the reunion. Because Andrew was like a brother to me, I knew we'd feel comfortable and both have fun.

As usual, I went to Lori's house unannounced. The house was deserted but her garden looked wonderful. *Maybe they're at the store or maybe they're working today or maybe they're off with the grandkids,* I thought. I decided to go back to Andrew's and call Lori later.

After calling several times, I finally reached her. I told her I'd be in town for only forty-eight hours and wanted to see her. She told me tonight wouldn't work, but agreed to meet for coffee at her house in the morning.

"That's kind of weird," I said to Andrew. "She's obviously got something going on tonight, but didn't tell me what . . . and that's not like Lori at all. Something's up with her. Well, I'll find out about it tomorrow."

"Maybe she's just preoccupied," Andrew said.

I glanced at him, "Yeah, maybe. Let's get going to the pre-reunion party, you ready?"

"Ready!"

After we dropped off Jennifer to Andrew's mother, who had offered to watch her, Andrew and I went to the party. Only a dozen people showed up, but the small gathering included the neighborhood boys Lori and I watched ride mini-bikes thirty-four years earlier. They still lived in Saginaw. They sure hadn't ventured very far. It made me aware that, despite the twists and turns life had dealt me, I had done okay for myself.

I didn't have a lot of time to spend with Lori the next morning, as I also wanted to take Jennifer to visit her grandmother's grave located in an old graveyard with gravel roads. While there, I promised to give her a quick driving lesson. As my smart little girl had so logically pointed out, it was the safest place to learn, because she couldn't kill anybody! Then I had the high school reunion to attend that evening. I looked forward to visiting with Lori and hoped we would be able to talk the way we used to.

I pulled the car into Lori's long gravel drive. Jennifer jumped out and had already knocked by the time I joined her at Lori's side door.

"Who is it?"

"It's us . . . Bonny and Jennifer!"

Lori opened the door, with Maggie in her arms. The dog barked, but Lori kept a firm grip. "Hi, Hon!" she said, holding open the storm door so we could slip past her.

"I'll put Maggie in the bathroom."

Jennifer and I sat at the kitchen table that Lori had covered with photographs of babies and toddlers.

"Give me a hug!" Lori demanded of Jennifer when she returned. "Gee, Bon, is she taller than you?"

I squeezed my daughter, and said, "Any day now she'll be looking down on her little mama." Lori and Jennifer both laughed.

"Let me get us some coffee. Jennifer, do you like coffee?"

"Yes, please," replied my daughter.

Lori handed us the coffee, then sat down at the table and told us about her neighbors she checked on, the boys at *Boysville*, and other tidbits. As I sat and listened and looked at Lori, I realized how much time had slipped by and how much I missed her! Lori's blond hair had turned mostly gray, but, unlike me, she didn't have any wrinkles. Her energy level, as usual, was off the charts.

Over the next hour, Lori went on and on about each grandchild pointing to the various pictures on the table. She shared little stories about each of them.

"Did I tell you Marie had another baby?"

"No . . ."

Lori handed me a photograph. "Oh, sorry, I meant to! Yes, two months ago, she had a little girl. She's named Katy." I glanced at the photograph as Lori continued. "And Ken, did I tell you about Ken?"

"The last thing I remember you mentioning about Ken was he'd moved back home."

"Well, yes, that was a long time ago. He's thinking of going on to college . . . *and* he's in love. I really like his girlfriend and I'm hoping for wedding bells very soon."

Lori also talked about her photography. She'd been taking lots of wonderful shots at parks, of nature during the changing seasons, and of Maggie. Then she asked about my father and how he was doing at his sister's home in Florida. Before we knew it, Jennifer and I had to leave.

After visiting mother's tombstone, I gave Jennifer her first driving lesson around the graveyard leaving me barely enough time to get my daughter over to Andrew's mother, before I raced over to Andrew's house to change for the reunion.

Thankfully, more people attended the reunion than the previous evening's get-together. Still, it didn't take Andrew and me long to make the rounds. A few classmates had gone on to be successful, but most were just middle-aged people who lived day-to-day and came to the reunion to relive life thirty years before. Sad, really. I decided this would be my last reunion.

We sat down at one of the tables to await our meal. "So how did your visit with Lori go?" Andrew asked.

"It was fun. She's gotten gray, which surprised me, but she's still a ball of energy and loves being a grandmother."

"I actually meant, did you find out what's up with her? I know you thought there's something wrong."

I took a sip of my wine. "No. Maybe it was because Jennifer was there, but Lori never brought up how she and Steve were doing . . . and I didn't ask."

"It's probably all in your mind. I'm sure she's fine."

"Yeah, you're probably right."

22
SHAMBLES

After returning to Texas, my life grew more stressful and hectic and eventually fell into complete shambles. I worked hard to single-handedly be a mother and father for my daughter. I know plenty of people do it every day, and before I married, I never thought twice about it. Lately, though, it seemed I never had enough time or money. Jennifer's biological father had been out of the picture since shortly after her birth and her stepfather—who at one point said he wanted to adopt her—had left our lives forever to start his new family. Of course, my father couldn't help in his condition.

Like my mother, I suffered from stress-triggered asthma. My health insurance coverage ended with my marriage, while the frequency of my attacks increased. I landed in the ICU several times. In order to pay the mounting medical bills, I ended up having to sell nearly everything I owned. The boat, the rental property, old computers, books, clothing, household items, the furniture, the house, and finally, my floundering business were all sold for much less than they were worth.

At forty-nine I had had everything I'd worked a lifetime to acquire. At fifty, the results of being hospitalized took it all away.

To add salt to the wound, a month later my precious cat, Inky, who I loved as much as Lori loved Maggie Mae, died in my arms. Inky and I had shared nineteen years together. I lost it. I needed Lori. I needed her to shake me out of this pity party where I found myself. I needed to talk with her.

"Hey, Bon, good to hear from you. I wanted to ask you something."

"Yeah? What?"

"Ken is getting married. Can you come home for it?"

Lori had no idea what I'd just gone through. "I'm so sorry, Lori, but I simply can't afford the trip. Tell Ken I'll be there in spirit." My heart was broken that I couldn't be there for my godson's wedding, but I was struggling just to keep my daughter and me fed.

With Lori so excited about the happy events in her life, I didn't want to bring her down by sharing mine.

"So what's up with you?" she asked.

I lied, "Same old stuff."

"How's Jennifer?"

"She's fine: getting straight A's. I'm so proud of her."

"She's a smart cookie, just like her mom."

"Thanks, Lor. Hey, I better get going, and I know you have tons to do with the upcoming wedding. Give Ken my love and blessings."

"Will do. Love ya."

"Love you too."

Several months after Ken's wedding, Lori called to share that one of her photographs had been selected for the cover of an upcoming YA mystery novel by a Canadian author.

I congratulated her. "How thrilling!"

"Yeah, it's kind of cool."

"What did you photograph?"

"Oh, it's a scene in a park near me. I played with it a little, so it looks darker and there's a light glowing from the back through the trees."

"You really do have an incredible gift for photography, Lori—a great eye for capturing unique scenes out of the ordinary." At that point the two cats my daughter and I recently rescued and adopted began a hissing argument, Jennifer yelled for me from her bedroom and my cell phone rang. My concentration splintered.

"Lor, I'm going to have to go. All hell is breaking lose here."

Lori laughed. "Okay, hon, just call me when you can."

"Will do." After things quieted down, I realized I'd forgotten to get the name of the book. I made a mental note to call Lori back to get the information to buy a copy when I could afford it.

CR80

I called Lori several times over the next year. Sometimes I reached Steve who told me she wasn't there, or just the answering machine. Lori did not return my calls. Maybe she was too busy with her kids and three grandkids. Or, maybe she had her own hell she was dealing with as well? I had no idea.

Through the help of a friend, I finally landed a job selling advertising . . . in San Diego. I was excited to leave this time. Over the past ten years in Texas I had gotten married, divorced, had huge success and dismal failures. It was time to move on.

My daughter was angry when I told her we were moving. "Mom, you are ruining my life! All my friends are here."

"You'll make new friends there, sweetie."

"I don't want new friends. I like my old friends."

I tried to appease her, "Look at it this way, you're not losing any friends, your doubling the number of friends you have. There's the Internet and Facebook, and, of course, the phone, so you can stay in touch as often as you want."

"I hate you."

I knew my daughter didn't mean it, she was just angry. "Yeah, yeah, go ahead. Hate me. We're still moving." I paused to think of something to make it easier for her. "How about if I talk with the color guard coach here to see about getting you on the team in San Diego?"

Jennifer compromised. "Okay."

As it turned out, the coach at her current high school had been college roommates with the coach at the high school she would be transferring to. Talk about a small world! Jennifer was accepted on the team, which helped alleviate some of the stress of moving.

So once again, I loaded up a twenty-six foot rented truck, tied down my car on the trailer behind it and drove my daughter, our kitties, and all our remaining belongings across country. Jennifer started her training for color guard the same day I started my new job. Within a month of our move, Jennifer started tenth grade in San Diego and had already made twenty close friends. Our new lives were off and running. I loved the weather and the beauty of San Diego, and I started making friends as well. Despite that, I desperately missed my best friend.

One Saturday I called Lor, expecting to get the answering machine, but she answered.

"Hey, Lor!"

"Bonny!"

"I've been trying to reach you for about a year! Where have you been?"

"Been busy between the kids and grandkids. What's up?"

"We moved . . . again. We're back in San Diego . . . and I'm loving it," I said as I looked from my balcony toward the Pacific Ocean.

Lori shared that she had two more grandchildren. Marie was now the mother of four, and Ken had recently become a daddy as well. She also announced that Ken attended college, studying to be a teacher. She was so proud.

"I've got some sad news, though."

"Oh no . . . what?" I asked.

"My mom's been diagnosed with lung cancer." Lori described how she and her siblings were helping with the trips to the doctors, etcetera. They were scared, yet, they all had faith she would come through.

I then asked how things were between her and Steve. She admitted they weren't great. Same stuff. She wanted him to talk to her more, to show some affection. He was too tired when he came home from work. They didn't even share the same bed anymore. I felt sad for Lori. I didn't know who had it worse: me, who hadn't had a man in years now; or to be in, what Lori perceived as, a one-sided relationship. Neither situation was good for the heart.

"I'm so glad Maggie is here with me. She's my best friend. We go on our long walks. She always agrees with everything I say and constantly kisses me. I don't know what I'd do without her." I heard Lori light up a cigarette before she asked, "So how is Jennifer doing?"

"Great. She loves it here, has made a ton of friends and is very involved in Color Guard."

"And your Dad?"

"As far as I know, he's okay. He never calls me and I only call him every few months. Last I heard, he's doing okay. Although, when Jennifer and I visited him over Christmas, his legs were pencil thin. He just won't get up and walk around. He lets his sister wait on him hand and foot. From the time he gets up to the time he goes to bed, he sits at the dining table and lets her bring him whatever he needs or wants."

"It's that generation, Bon."

"Yeah, I suppose your right. I'm glad he has his sister, but I think not getting any exercise is going to hurt him in the end."

"And, lastly, how are you?"

"Okay, working long hours, trying to make sales, just to keep the rent paid. It's so expensive here, Lor."

"But you love it, remember?"

I smiled. "Yes, you are right. I do love it."

For over two hours we had our heart-to-heart talk I had missed so much over the past several years. We had talked about life, about God, about our pets, about death, about love, about it all. We had caught up. Our conversation had been food to my soul.

23
CHANGES

Lori called me about a month later. "What's up in your world, Lori?"

Silence.

"Lori?"

Finally, she spoke, but I could tell she had been crying. "I'm going to divorce Steve."

I'd known for awhile she was not happy, but she usually didn't want to talk about it. Instead Lori focused on her children, stepchildren and grandchildren to avoid the problem. Maybe it had become unbearable—as my marriage had. "What? After all this time? Why?"

"He doesn't love me. He never talks to me, he won't listen to me, he doesn't even sleep with me. I'm sure there's someone out there better for me."

"Lor, I'm so sorry. But, seriously, you better think about this long and hard. Steve has been with you for over twenty years. He's been there to raise your kids as his own, he's provided you a home, he loves you Lori, though he may not show it the way you want him to." I took a breath. "Lor, being a divorcée is not all it's cracked up to be. Seriously. Any available guys our age, well there's a reason they're single. Either they're gay or just plain weird. The pickings are not good. Otherwise, why would I still be single after all these years?"

Lori began going on and on about Steve, growing louder and louder. Then I heard his voice in the background telling her to shut up. She wouldn't. It finally dawned on me, Lori was drunk on her butt. I let her rant and rave for a short while, but there was no way I could talk with her over a phone at this point. She wouldn't listen, nor would she remember our discussion. I ended the conversation and told her I'd call her back tomorrow.

During the night, I thought about options for Lori and what I could do to help her. I decided the best course of action would be to fly her out to stay with me for a week. That would clear her head and give her a fresh perspective. I called Lori the next day to tell her that.

"Lor, I really think this would help. A lot. New scenery, new place, it will give you a new point of view, and hopefully the answers you're looking for. I'll pay for your ticket and feed you. Will you come?"

"Thanks, Bon, but I can't."

"Do you mean you can't or won't? What is stopping you from coming out? It's only seven days out of your life and it could be exactly what you need."

"No, I don't like traveling. I'm terrified of flying. I just can't."

"Okay, so you've never flown. You might like it."

"No."

"Okay, how about the Amtrak? That would be a lot of fun seeing the country. It will take three days to get here, but it also gives you lots of time to think."

"No, I'd go crazy. Claustrophobic, you know."

"Right." I thought a moment. *How in the world could I get her out here?* My ideas dried up.

"Well, Lori, I really don't know what to do. You won't fly or ride the train, the Greyhound Bus would be worse . . . and with Jennifer in school, I can't just jump on a plane to come take you away."

"Don't worry about it," Lori said. "I've got my mom here. I'll figure out how to handle things. I'm just miserable and this has got to stop."

"Lor, I love you. You know that?"

"Yeah."

"That means, if you want or need to talk, morning or night, call me, okay?"

"Okay."

"By the way, how's your mom?"

"She's in remission."

"That's awesome!"

"Yeah, we're all pretty relieved, and that's the biggest reason I don't want to go anywhere."

Now, I completely understood. Lori was a lot closer to her family. I didn't feel like I even had a family most of the time, except for my daughter. "I understand. No problem, Lor. Love you."

"Love you, too."

I worried that Lori may start the binge drinking again. I made a pledge to myself to stay in contact with her as much as possible.

Bonny Brookes

24
SUPPORT

L ori and I stayed in touch on a regular basis—either by phone, email or Facebook. We had both joined the high tech world of our children . . . and our children taught us how to use these communication tools.

Back in high school, Lori and I were amazed at how much the world had changed in our grandparents' lifetimes. They had lived through two world wars, the invention of automobiles, women earning the right to vote, the invention of refrigerators, phones becoming common in homes, the invention of radios and eventually television. Now, as Lori and I looked back over our lives, we realized how much had changed: the invention of color TV, man walking on the moon, computers, cell phones, the Internet, iPads, texting and video phones. What would our children experience? It was beyond our imagination. The one thing we were sure of, the world was changing at warp speed.

ᏟᎦᎬᎴ

I relaxed in my lounge chair on the balcony under a blue, cloudless California sky. With a notebook balanced on my knees, and a pen held in the air, I thought about what to write in my annual Christmas letter. As my mind wandered back over the last year, I had a strong impulse to call Lori.

"Hey Lor, you were on my mind . . . so, Hi!"

"Oh, that is so *weird*, I just reached for the phone to call you!"

I laughed. "Great minds think alike! So what's up?"

"Well, I know you probably can't come out for it, but Ken is graduating from college. He's getting his degree in Education. I'm so happy and proud!"

"Lor, I'm so proud of both of you! For you, as the mom that hung in there, despite the odds; and for him to go after his dreams. Ken has really matured into a wonderful young man, father and husband!"

"Yes he has! I'll be sure to send you pictures . . . unless you can come?"

There was no way. I just couldn't afford the time or money for the trip. "I'm sorry, Lor, I just can't. Please give Ken a giant bear hug for me and tell him it's from his *Aunt* Bonny."

"And when you see him next time, you can give him another," Lori said.

"Will do." I felt rather guilty because I had missed Ken's high school graduation, his wedding and now his college graduation. Being so far apart had a downside.

"So are things better between you and Steve?"

Without hesitation, Lori answered. "Yes, and thanks for hanging in there and talking with me when I needed you."

"You were there for me. I just returned the favor, Lor. So what happened?"

"Well, you know, I thought he didn't love me anymore, because he never wanted to talk to me and it seemed, not even be with me. But that wasn't the case at all. He was just too tired. So we started having our 'date' days again, and it's like we're newly married. I'm in love and loved and I couldn't be happier."

"I'm so glad you had a better ending than I did."

"Me, too. Steve's a good guy, and I'd be a fool to leave him."

Lori and I talked for a few more minutes before I went back to work on my Christmas letters.

25
TEACHER

Lori called me a few months later, crying. "Bon . . ."

"Lori? Lori what is it? Is it your mom?"

After a few moments of swallowing down her sobs, Lori finally answered. "No . . . it's Maggie. My little Maggie Mae has gone to God."

"Oh, Lori. I'm so sorry. I know how much you loved Maggie." In my mind, I visualized Lori tightly holding Maggie and how fiercely protective Maggie was of Lori when Jennifer and I visited. I understood how deep this hurt Lori. "She's with God now, Lori . . . and when it's your turn, she'll be waiting there for you."

Lori took a deep, unsteady breath. "Do you really think so?"

"I know so." I sat down at my computer and pulled up a document. "Lor, I want to send you something that might help your pain. Are you near your computer?"

"Yes."

"Great, I'm going to send you a poem right now . . . this is for you and Maggie. It helped me when I lost Inky. Let's read it together while we're on the phone. Are you willing?"

"Okay."

I quickly emailed the poem by an unknown author.

"I got it, Bon."

"Okay, open it and let's read it together."

I began, *"The Rainbow Bridge,"* and then Lori joined in.

> *"Just this side of heaven is a place called Rainbow Bridge. When an animal dies that has been especially close to someone here, that pet goes to Rainbow Bridge."*

I went silent to let Lori continue at her own pace.

> *"There are meadows and hills for all of our special friends so they can run and play together. There is plenty of food, water and sunshine and our friends are warm and comfortable.*
>
> *"All the animals who had been ill and old are restored to health and vigor; those who were hurt or maimed are made whole and strong again."*

Lori stopped a moment. I could feel the peace the poem brought to her. She continued:

> *"Just as we remember them in our dreams of days and times gone by, the animals are happy and content, except for one small thing: they each miss someone very special to them, who had to be left behind.*
>
> *"They all run and play together, but the day comes when one suddenly stops and looks into the distance. His bright eyes are intent; his eager body begins to quiver. Suddenly, he begins to run from the group, flying over the green grass, his legs carrying him faster and faster."*

Lori stopped as sobs overtook her.

As I listened to her cry, my own eyes filled with tears. I swiped them away. "Take a minute if you need to, Lor. This will help. I promise you." Lori continued reading.

> *"You have been spotted, and when you and your special friend finally meet, you cling together in joyous reunion, never to be parted again. The happy kisses rain upon your face, your hands again caress the beloved head, and you look once more into the trusting eyes of your pet, so long gone from your life, but never absent from your heart."*

I joined Lori in reading the last line:

> *"Then you cross the Rainbow Bridge together."*

Lori took a deep breath. "That's beautiful. Thanks, Bonny."

CR80

Andrew and I stayed in touch via email and phone calls and one Friday afternoon, I called him and learned his mother was in the hospital. That prompted me to call my father. He hadn't called me in years, and I only called him every month or so. His sister answered the phone and casually told me, "Oh, he's in the hospital."

"What? Why didn't you call? What happened?"

"I didn't think you needed to know. He fell. He has diabetes and his foot has a bad infection."

I called the hospital and couldn't believe what happened next. The person at the other end of the line informed me, without a Power of Attorney, I needed a personal identification number. His sister couldn't find the number when I called her back. My father was in the hospital and strangers prevented me from even talking with him!

After hanging up with my aunt, I paced the floor in outrage. Then I thought about Lori and her mother. She would understand the fear I felt, since her mother was ill as well. Even though it was late, I decided to call her.

"My mom is doing really well, actually. We're all so relieved," Lori said.

Then I got a little choked up and told her about my father. Lori loved him about as much as I did and started crying.

"Oh, Bon. I'm so sorry. What can I do? Why won't they let you talk with him? You're his next of kin, not your aunt."

Lori was right. Since his divorce, as the oldest child, I was my father's next of kin. That made me even angrier.

"I don't know, Lori. I'm going to have to fly to Florida to take care of things. He doesn't have a will or Power of Attorney or anything. Man, I can't believe this. If he had taken care of himself, walked every day, rather than have his sister attend to his every need, he would have gotten more exercise and wouldn't be in this situation. It's sad, but he brought it upon himself."

"I'm sorry, Bonny," Lori said again. "Call me when you get back from Florida, and tell him I love him."

"I will, Lor . . . and thanks for listening to me rant."

"That's what friends are for! Love you."

26
FAMILY FEUD

Because Martha lived closer to the nursing home and could help Father if he needed it, it made sense to list both of us as co-POA's. However, she refused to sign the co-POA and only agreed to a Power of Attorney listing her as lead, with me as back-up. She was my aunt, and I trusted her, so I didn't have a problem with this.

That changed when I arrived in Florida in April to visit my father and stayed with Aunt Martha. After I'd been there a few days, I watched her write a thousand dollar check from my father's account and deposit it into her own account. When I asked what she was doing, she explained it was to pay some of his bills.

"What? Why don't you just pay the bills directly from his checking account?"

She turned away from me and from over her shoulder said, "That's not the way I do things."

"Well, that's the way it is supposed to be done. Otherwise that's fraud."

"I'm not doing anything wrong, and who's going to say anything anyway?" She sat down on the sofa and starting working on her word puzzles.

I began to question my complete faith in her. I knew the VA covered most of my father's bills. "Let me see the bills."

She pointed to them as if she had nothing to hide and I looked them over. I pointed out that the bills only totaled three hundred dollars and asked what the other seven hundred dollars was for that she'd taken from his account. She ignored my question and focused on her puzzle.

She was my aunt and I couldn't believe she'd be malicious or embezzle from her brother, so I dropped it for the time being. I needed to return home to my daughter, so left the following day.

Two months later, I flew cross-country to visit my father again. The first morning I walked into the nursing home, I spotted him in his wheelchair at a table in the "social hall." Eager to see him, I quickly approached and said hi before bending over to kiss his cheek. He turned his head away and accused me of stealing his money. I was shocked, especially since the only person who had access to his money was his sister, not me. I began seriously suspecting Aunt Martha was up to no good. That evening I asked her why he would think that. She only laughed and said it was due to his dementia. Again, I let it go, hoping I was wrong, but in my gut I knew she was up to something.

During August, I wrote Martha asking her to mail me an accounting of Father's resources. A month passed and still she had not done so. So, I called her to ask for it again, she flatly refused saying she was the one taking care of him and it wasn't my business.

Then she asked if I planned to move him to a nursing home in San Diego. The question appalled me. Father had become so frail—she of all people knew that—so she knew he wasn't in any condition to be moved across the country! Her behavior annoyed me and made me question her motives for offering to help with my father. I didn't dignify her question with a real answer.

I began calling my father weekly and taking detailed notes.

In early October, I called to speak to him and one of the nursing home attendants explained that gangrene had developed in Father's leg and he was at the hospital to have it amputated. I immediately called the hospital, but despite speaking to several nurses, including the head nurse, they all refused to give me any information unless I could provide a personal identification number.

"No, I don't have a PIN, but I am his closest kin: his eldest child, and further, I'm on the POA."

"Well, I'm looking at the POA and your name is nowhere to be found," the woman informed me.

What? I told the nurse I'd call back. If I was a cartoon character, steam would have been pouring out my ears as I dialed my aunt's phone number.

"Why wasn't I told Dad went to the hospital to have his leg amputated?"

"It must have slipped my mind."

"Yeah, okay." I didn't believe her. "Well, the hospital won't let me talk with him without a pin. Do you have it?"

"Somewhere around here." I heard her rustling through papers and then she gave me the number.

"By the way, do you know why I need a PIN?"

Martha scoffed, almost as if I'd just asked the world's dumbest question. "So you can talk to your Dad, of course."

"Could it be because I'm no longer on the POA?"

Several moments of silence slipped by before she responded, "I didn't want you on there."

"Did you forget it is not *your* POA? I'm sure Dad doesn't even realize what you've done, does he? Do I need to contact an attorney?"

"Do what you want," she said and then hung up.

I sent Lori an email giving her an update of my father's condition. Within minutes her response came:

Oh Bonny. I'm so very sad right now. Please, please, please take care. I had no idea that your dad was that ill. Sending you big hugs and I will be praying for your dad and you. Moments like this make me wish that we lived closer because I want to be there for you. Spiritually I am though, and the way I feel right now inside, well you know. God bless you, my dear friend.

Now, I'm in tears. I normally don't dream that much, but last night I truly had a dream with both you and Andrew in it—all three of us were at his parent's yellow farmhouse. I've had both you and Andrew on my mind lately. You're not alone Bonny, nor is your dad. God LOVES YOU . . . and so do I!

Tears rolled down my face. "And, Lor, I love you."

I decided to seek legal council. I just needed to make sure father was okay and I had all the facts straight first.

The day after my father was released from the hospital, I called him and asked how he felt and if he needed anything. He told me he was fine and he sounded good, so I went on to ask him why he changed the POA.

"What? I didn't change anything."

Bingo. My gut feeling had been right: Martha changed the POA without my father's direction, knowledge or agreement. How in the hell she got away with it, I'll never know.

After hanging up with my father, I released my pent-up anger and frustration with a stream of profanities. That, of course, caused Jennifer to come running out of her bedroom to check on me.

"Mom?"

"Oh, sorry, babe. I'm just so ticked off!"

"What's wrong?"

Jennifer, who was now a mature high school senior, had not seen her grandfather in several years and had met her great-aunt only twice. I debated whether to tell her, but then decided to be candid.

"Your Great-Aunt Martha. She seems to think just because your grandfather has lived with her for a few years, all he has is now hers. She's saying, 'He didn't want to live with you. He doesn't like you. I'm the one who took care of him for the past eight years. I'll notify you if you need to know something—'"

"Wait a minute, Mom, I remember us wanting Grandpa to live with us. We even had that extra bedroom set up for him. Didn't *she* convince him to stay with her?"

"Grandpa said Texas was too hot, but yeah, he didn't want to go to Florida either—she convinced him." I stroked back some loose blonde hairs out of my daughter's face. "She has control of everything and is doing her best to push us out of his life and poison his mind against us." I dabbed at tears welling up in the inner corners of my eyes, "Grandpa had his leg amputated."

My daughter wrapped her arms around me and squeezed me, while laying her head on my shoulder. "Mom, Grandpa will be okay . . . and she's a bitch."

I immediately clenched Jennifer's forearms, tilting her away from me as I looked into her eyes. "What did you just say?"

"Well, Mom, you said it . . . I thought it was okay." Then a half-grin appeared on her lips. "Anyway, she is."

"I don't approve of the language, and more than that, I don't want my anger to warp your impression of your great-aunt."

"Mom, it's okay."

I drew my daughter in for another hug. "Thanks, Baby. I'm going to call Lori now. She always helps me to calm down and see things in a better light."

Jennifer leaned away, "And I don't?"

"Honey, you're wonderful, but I don't want to burden you. Okay?"

Jennifer nodded, squeezed me and then returned to her bedroom to read the latest *Harry Potter* book.

I stood there, feeling powerless. Aunt Martha filled my father's head with lies, wouldn't keep me updated on his health and had taken control of his money. I didn't want my ranting to Lori to disturb Jennifer's reading, so I grabbed the phone and stepped out onto the balcony, barely noticing the beautiful, balmy October weather.

After saying hello, I began venting. "If I hadn't been calling Dad weekly, I wouldn't have even known he had gone to the hospital to have his leg amputated! And, the hospital wouldn't even let me talk to him without a damn PIN!"

"Maybe, Bon, your aunt's just so wrapped up in the day-to-day that she forgot. She's not young, you know."

"Yes, she's not young. But to forget about someone's leg being amputated? Forget about changing another person's POA? These are not little inconsequential details! I never dreamed she'd be so dishonest—she's family. If you can't trust your own family, who can you trust?"

My hands shook with rage as I stopped to light a cigarette. After exhaling, I relished the brief calmness smoking provided before setting the cigarette in the ashtray and continued my tirade. "Yes, she's forgetful about some things. However, I don't think it's forgetfulness, Lori, because she didn't just drop me off the POA. She added my cousin's girlfriend!"

I stood up and started pacing back and forth on the balcony. "Dad's blind! He can't see what his sister asked him to sign. He trusts her implicitly. She didn't even tell him what he signed. Otherwise, how come he didn't know and told me he hadn't signed a new POA?"

In an even, but firm tone, Lori asked, "Have you tried talking *calmly* to your aunt? Maybe there are things you're not aware of?"

My nerves were fried. I stopped pacing to stub out the cigarette I'd left burning in the ashtray, then lit a new one and returned to pacing back and forth on the balcony.

"I have tried. I knew she was hiding something. I just knew it." I sat back down in the chair, trying to gain control of my temper.

"Bon, have you ever thought that maybe she thinks she deserves what she took, because of all the years of care she's given him?"

"I'm sure she does, but Dad's been giving her rent money and buying her things all along. He's been taking care of her financially." I took a deep drag on my cigarette but it no longer relaxed me. "I need a beer."

"Oh, Bon, who would have ever thought she would be capable of such a scheme?"

"I sure didn't. Now I know why my mother never liked her, though." I crushed out my cigarette.

"What about your brother, Bon? What does he say about all this?"

"I wouldn't know. I've been calling and sending him emails. He doesn't respond." I took a deep breath, really wanting a drink. "I'm sorry, Lori, for dumping this on you. I thought getting it out would help, but it's not. I'm going to go have a beer."

"Just don't have too many. Call me if you need to talk more, okay?"

"Yep . . . and thanks."

"That's what friends are for."

CR&O

The nightmare continued. I contacted several attorneys, but unfortunately, none would take the case on contingency. In the end, I filed a complaint with the Attorney General. That didn't help either. It looked like Father's older sister would get away with everything she'd done.

My father's health continued to worsen. The doctors amputated his remaining foot and eventually his remaining leg. My aunt no longer communicated with me. I suppressed the stress, anger and hurt causing my asthma to flare up. I knew I needed to let my feelings out or I'd end up in the hospital.

As usual, I called Lori to vent.

"And now my dad's heath has really gone downhill. His mind comes in and out of reality, which, I guess, is good. I mean at least he doesn't know where he is. I need to get back to Florida to straighten this crap out, but I can't. I can't take anymore time off from work and Jennifer's high school graduation is right around the corner. I can't leave her to fend for herself. Lor, what should I do?"

"You are doing what you need to do. Don't feel guilty for being a good mom, Bon. Jennifer needs to come first to everything, including your dad. I think he'd understand."

"Yeah, but, I don't want that bitch to get away with this . . . and time is running out."

"Karma."

"So I should let the universe take care of it?"

"Yes. Karma will take care of his sister. Don't waste your energy."

I thanked Lori. She always said the right words to help me get some distance from the situation and calm down.

C380

Two more months passed by. I continued calling my father weekly. His voice grew fainter and fainter, and his mind wandered more and more. Occasionally, he'd be lucid, but more often, he imagined himself on a cruise ship or at war.

Despite the amputations, the gangrene continued to spread throughout his body. I kept Lori abreast of the situation and she always helped me to find the bright side.

Jennifer, because she hadn't been close to her grandfather, didn't appear too upset. She was more concerned about her high school graduation coming up in June.

On the last day of April, the hospital called to tell me Father needed to go into hospice care and they needed my permission. It seemed they finally figured out that I, not his sister, was Father's next of kin. Or maybe, Father's sister had refused to give consent. I didn't know.

I'd heard of hospice, but didn't know what it involved, so I asked.

"Your father is at the point where medication will never cure him, so, in hospice, all medication is stopped and the feeding tubes and IV's are removed."

"Oh." I visualized my father in various stages in his life: when I was a young girl and thought my daddy was the best guy in the world; when I was a teenager and so angry with him when I moved out; when Jennifer was an infant and he carried her around in the papoose as the proud Grandpa; and finally, the last time I had seen him in the nursing home nearly a year ago.

And then, I saw Mom waiting for him. I wiped away my tears and nodded, "Okay. Will you call me immediately if anything happens, good or bad?"

The nurse promised she would call.

A few hours later, I called to speak with Father. The nurse said he had been unresponsive for a few days, but she'd hold the phone to his ear.

"Dad . . . Daddy, this is Bonny. I just wanted you to know I love you."

The nurse came back on. "He heard you! He moaned and reached for the phone."

It made me feel better that he still recognized me. That night, I tossed and turned as questions crossed my mind. *What if he really isn't that sick? What if he slowly starves to death because they removed his feeding tube?* I decided to call the hospital as soon as I woke up.

I didn't get the chance. The phone rang at six in the morning—the same time it had rung thirty-eight years earlier about my mother. But, it wasn't the hospital calling, it was Martha. Father had died several hours before. Why hadn't the hospital called me? Why did his sister wait so long to call? It really didn't matter now, I guess.

But, the worse part came next. My cousin's girlfriend, the replacement POA, came on the line and told me, "You're unwanted and unwelcome because of all the stress you put your poor aunt through!"

I couldn't believe it. *Were they telling me not to come to my father's funeral? How dare they!*

I left my brother several phone messages and sent emails asking him to contact me immediately. He did not respond, leaving me no choice but to deal with this on my own.

Although I knew this day would come, to realize I would never speak with my father or see him again devastated me. If I went to Florida, it would be an ugly scene I didn't want to deal with. That meant I wouldn't even be there to say good-bye to my daddy one last time. I contacted the funeral home and arranged to listen to the service over the phone.

Then I contacted the bank, only to learn Father's sister had added her name to Father's bank accounts, so upon his death all his money reverted to her. She had broken the law, yet again! I could fight her, take her to court, and possibly get her put in jail for fraud and theft; but the ugliness of the whole situation, it was just too much. I didn't have the energy to talk, so I sent Lori an email letting her know my father had passed.

For the next two weeks, I bottled up my emotions, worked long days and ate little to nothing. My body finally rebelled with a full-blown asthma attack late one afternoon.

Jennifer knew I was not well. "Mom, do you need to go to the hospital?"

I looked at my seventeen-year-old daughter. Worry filled her big, dark-brown eyes. I thought briefly to myself, *I can't leave her the way my mother left me. I need to hang on.* Without enough air to speak, I simply nodded my head.

As my daughter drove me to the hospital, I went into convulsions before slipping into unconsciousness. The doctors pronounced me unresponsive upon arrival, and for the next week, I remained in a coma, on life support.

Once home from the hospital, I barely had the energy to stand up straight and had lost my voice, due to the pipes being shoved down my throat. I could no longer work at my sales job and found myself unemployed, unable to speak, and saddled with thousands of dollars of medical bills not covered by insurance.

Jennifer had called to give Lori updates several times during and after my hospital stay. Dozens of emails from Lori filled my inbox telling me how much she loved me, how worried she was and that she knew I'd come through this, like I always did—better and stronger than ever. I read her emails in silence. They uplifted me, yet I didn't have the energy to write back.

I finally called Lori just days before Jennifer's high school graduation. I thought I could whisper loud enough to be heard, but Lori couldn't understand me. I told her, as best I could, that I'd email her until my voice returned.

Within minutes of hanging up, I received Lori's email:

> *It's times like these that I wish I lived closer! Make you some meals and just help! I am so sorry that you're going through this, Bonny. You're on my mind so much. I truly believe that God is with you and lift you in my prayers, a lot! Rest, rest, rest! Easier said than done, I'm sure, but try not to over do it. I love you, Bonny! Stay in close contact w/me. Write me daily, if you want. I am HERE!!!! And, God is with you . . . hang on to knowing that he is!!!*
>
> *Love and Hugs,*
> *Lori*

Tears slipped down my cheeks. *What would I do without you, my precious, beloved friend?*

27
THE GRADUATE

The day before Jennifer's graduation, she received a card and check from Lori. Graduation morning, Lori called and wished my daughter well and good luck and told her she really wished she could be there.

That was Lori—always so thoughtful, sweet, generous and wishing the best for everyone.

After Jennifer's graduation—which took about all the strength I had just to attend—I knew things would never be the same for me. My daughter had been awarded a nearly-full scholarship to an exclusive private university, a godsend, yet that meant she would soon leave to begin her college career.

My current lease had ended and the rent was being jacked up to over two thousand dollars a month. Without a job, as much as I hated to leave, I didn't know how I could stay. In just eight short weeks, my whole life had changed. I felt I'd completely lost control for the first time ever. Worse, any hope I held for the future, had completely vanished.

That's when the angels, in the form of friends, intervened. One offered to let me stay at his place. All I needed to do was return to Texas—that meant loading up all my belongings on a rented moving truck and driving over fifteen-hundred miles. But first, I needed to get my daughter settled into the next chapter of her life.

In early August, I held a brave front as I moved Jennifer into her dormitory. When I returned to my car and closed the door, however, I broke down in uncontrollable, body-heaving, sobs.

After several minutes, I told myself, *Enough of this! You need to load up the truck, the cats and begin the journey back to Texas.*

I reached for a tissue, dried my eyes and blew my nose, then started the ignition. As I drove away, I watched Jennifer's college grow smaller in the rearview mirror. Tears overtook me again. Despite how much I loved San Diego and how terribly much I'd miss my baby girl; I had no other choice but to leave.

CR&O

In mid-August I arrived in the Austin area with a broken heart and crushed dreams. One evening I posted some photos of me in my new surroundings on Facebook, so Lori and Jennifer would see that I was doing okay.

"I'm thinking about going back to school to get my teaching certificate—to teach kindergarten," I told Lori when she called a week later.

"Really? Isn't that what you originally went to college for, but switched to business?"

"Yes, but, you know, for the life of me, I can't remember why I switched. I guess too many years have slipped by."

"Well, I think you'll make a great teacher. Good plan, Bon! Things seem to be working out for you there and that makes me real happy."

"Thanks, Lor. I really appreciate your support."

"I am so happy that you're doing better! I'm giving you a big hug! Do you feel it?"

I laughed. "Not quite, but thanks for the thought."

"You know, my heart smiled when I saw the pictures you posted on Facebook."

"You know, *now*, I'm okay?" I always enjoyed teasing Lori. "Didn't you believe me?"

"I believed you, but it's hard to explain, Bonny. I know you really liked living in California, but I just envision Texas as your home. You have returned there, my friend, on more than one occasion. Who knows, maybe you'll stay put this time."

"Maybe."

"I'm glad Jennifer likes college. It really sounds like you've made several good changes. I am so sincerely happy for you both!"

"Thanks, Lor. What would I do without you cheering in my corner? So how are you doing?"

Lori told me about her photography. The book sporting one of her photographs on the cover, *The Ghost of Colby Drive,* had finally been published and was available online now.

"That's so cool! I'm going to buy one, and the next time I see you, I want you to autograph it, okay?"

Lori giggled. "It's not that big of a deal, but okay." Lori's energy level rose when she changed the subject to her six grandchildren and all their adventures. It seemed she was surrounded by her family every day.

Lori stopped to cough, took a breath and then in a softer, tone, told me about Marie's new beau.

"What a minute. Did I miss something . . . like a divorce?"

"Oh, Bonny. Yes, I didn't want to tell you with all the stuff you were going through with your dad. Yeah, Marie got divorced over a year ago."

"Well, as long as she's happy. I'm glad she's met someone else. She's still young and pretty. It's been so long for me, I kind of doubt I'll ever meet anyone."

"Oh, you will! Did I tell you Ken is still searching for a teaching job?"

"Really, I thought he'd have found one by now."

"Yeah, that's what we all thought. But with the economy and the budget cuts, he's having a hard time."

"Man, that sucks. I'm sure he'll find one eventually. But, hearing that, maybe I should rethink my teaching plan. It's food for thought."

"Maybe the job market there is different, Bon. Go for your dreams." Lori hopped happily from one topic to the next for several minutes.

"So, Lori, how are you and Steve doing?"

"We're good, real good. I actually feel closer to him with each passing day."

I was thrilled to hear it.

28
SOUL SHARING

The place I originally moved to after leaving San Diego, reeked of gasoline from the scooters my friend kept in the garage. The fumes were so toxic to my weak lungs that I ended up back in the hospital for a week with pneumonia. Once again, my energy was depleted and now I had even more hospital debt that I simply couldn't pay. To add salt to the wound, my request for financial assistance was denied.

I moved into the vacation home of my daughter's godfather. Built into the side of rocky hills, the small two-bedroom condo provided views of Lake Travis and the Texas Hill Country as far as the eye could see. I felt very blessed and lucky to live in such beautiful surroundings. However, it had three major drawbacks: the condo was an hour out of town; there was no garage; and it required climbing up forty steps from the parking lot to my bedroom.

The stairs knocked the wind out of me and I ended up back in the hospital, but only for a day this time.

I leaned back against the pillows on top of my bed and gazed out the window at the gorgeous view. Trees, in shades of red, gold and green covered the hills. I stared at the sunlight dancing across the dark blue waters of the lake, yet, barely noticed it. My depression grew with each passing day. I'd worked all my life to build good credit, save money, give my daughter a good life, and then I got sick and everything I worked for was gone. Only in America.

Normally, with Christmas only two weeks away, I'd be filled with anticipation, but not this year. My daughter was in California and, for the first time, we wouldn't be spending the holiday together. Any hope I held for the future, had evaporated.

The phone on the bedside table rang. I reached over for it, then reclined back against my pillows and looked back out the window as I answered. A familiar voice greeted me.

"Lori?" I sat up straighter and felt excitement flow through me. "Lori, it's so good to hear your voice! I was sitting here feeling sorry for myself . . . and then you call." If anyone could help me get out of this funk, Lori could. "I already feel better!"

"First, *Happy Birthday!* and second, I've been worried about you, Bonny. You've been in the hospital so much." Lori then started coughing uncontrollably. She sounded horrible.

"Lori, are you okay?"

"Yeah, just a cold."

"You sound terrible. Are you still smoking?"

"Oh, it's just a cold . . . or something. No big deal."

"Are you still smoking?"

"Yeah, I'm entitled to one vice, aren't I?"

"I suppose so, but you really don't sound good. Please take care of yourself, because if you don't, how can you take care of anyone else?"

"I'm fine, Bon. Did you quit?"

"Yeah, over seven months ago. So what's up with you?"

"I was calling to wish you happy birthday, happy holidays and catch up." Lori and I began telling each other about what had been going on for the past several months.

"Climbing up these stairs, with a depleted immune system, literally knocked the air out of me. I had to go to the ER for a breathing treatment, and guess what?"

"What?"

"The bill came up to eleven-thousand dollars!"

"*What?*"

"Yep. The charges were grossly excessive. Just to draw blood, the charge was over a thousand. Can you believe it?"

"Oh my God! This is why I don't go to doctors. Did I tell you that Steve's employer stopped providing insurance?"

"No . . . why?"

"Because the premium rates were spiking, yet the coverage was dropping. It was either cut the wages or drop the insurance. They dropped the insurance. So now, we're in your boat without insurance. So, I guess, if we get sick and end up in the hospital, if we don't die, the debt kills us."

"Yep. Sad, but oh-so-true."

I told Lori how much Jennifer liked college, but I missed her terribly—I wouldn't see her again until the following summer. Lori brought me up-to-date on her grandchildren's school activities. She told me how much she loved spending time with them, playing games, and creating and hanging decorations for Christmas. "They keep me young!"

I laughed. "Lori, you're not old. But, on the other hand, I know little ones have energy levels off the charts, so they must keep you running!"

"They do, but I love it." Lori stopped as she had another coughing fit.

"Lori?"

"I'm okay," she said. "Damn cold. Anyway, I've been taking lots of photos . . . mainly the grandkids, but also some nature shots. I'm pretty proud of them."

"I'd love to see them, Lori."

"I'll post them on Facebook soon." Lori's voice changed to a whisper, "And, now for the big news . . ."

Not knowing what she was being secretive about, my curiosity rose. "What?"

"Steve and I are considering adopting a new puppy from the pound."

I whooped with glee and congratulated her. I knew how much joy a dog would bring her.

"Bon?" Lori's voice had suddenly switched from jovial to very serious. Again I wondered if something was wrong.

"Yes?"

"Remember that summer—forty years ago—when we read the Bible?"

"Of course, Lori!"

"Well, remember the Book of Revelation, and how we talked about the world coming to an end in our generation or our children's . . . and back then, we made a pact to not have children?"

"Yeah, so much for keeping that vow."

"Yeah." Lori went quiet for a moment then continued. "Bon, I am seeing stuff happening that's in the Revelation. This country is falling apart, which is just what the Bible said, and our president . . . well, I think he's the devil incarnate. He has a whole hidden agenda, and is moving one step at a time, like a wolf reining in the lambs. He is dumbing down this country and systematically taking away our rights one by one until all hope is gone."

I thought about what Lori said. "These are scary times in many, many ways. So many people are unemployed, small businesses, who are the biggest creators of new jobs, are being taxed right out of business, so more people lose their jobs, and then they can't afford to buy things beyond basic necessities, only crippling the economy more. It's a ripple effect through the nation."

"Yeah, and now I hear employers are required to offer insurance if they have so many full-time employees, and so lots of employers here are cutting the hours below full-time," Lori said. "That means employees now work fewer hours so their income is less, yet they're expected to pay more for insurance? And, if they don't, they get fined by the government, and may even go to jail down the road."

"Not logical is it. You disobey the law, you go to jail because you can't afford the insurance premiums, and now you are punished with free housing, food and medical care! What kind of message is that?"

Lori snorted. "It's ludicrous. And, the mandatory government-run medical program, that's about insurance companies getting richer, not about improving the medical care in this country and that definitely should not be run by the government. And, if it's such a great program, why are the politicians exempt?"

"Good point," I said.

"Oh, I found out chances are we won't even qualify for this new program. I wonder if you will?"

"That's uplifting. Not! I'll have to check into it." My frustration with anything medical led to anger these days and I needed to change the subject. "Anyway, I'm afraid our country's glory days are behind us."

"Hey Bon, hang on a second, I want to go get some more coffee." In seconds, Lori was back on the line and said in a serious voice. "I want to ask you something that I've had on my mind, but I'm not sure how to."

Lori usually didn't have problems asking me things, which made me wonder what it could be. "Just say it."

"Bon, when you were in your coma, did you see anything?"

"Why are you asking that, Lori? Is something going on with you? Your cough does *not* sound good."

"No, I'm okay. I'm just curious."

"Well, yeah, I saw stuff . . . but I think the drugs brought it on. I told my daughter. Of course, she laughed and told me I was nuts."

"Tell me about it. Weren't there other times when you saw stuff as well? Did you see the same things each time?"

"I have had these visions a total of three times, Lori. And, no, none of the experiences have been the same. I don't share these things, because I don't want others to think I'm loony."

"I don't think you're crazy, Bon, I think you have a special knowing. Please tell me about one of the times."

"Well, okay. The first time I was seventeen years old, just four months after my mom passed. Since the day my mom died, I had dreams about her every night and felt like she came to me and we talked. On those occasions, I didn't want to wake up, because then I knew Mom wouldn't be there. But this time, there was a difference."

"How?"

"Well, Andrew and I were over at a friend's house and I had an asthma attack—and despite taking my inhaler—it just continued to get worse. I told Andrew I was going to go lie down. He's always been such a sweet guy."

"Yep, good ole' Andrew. Sorry, keep going."

"Anyway, he got down on the floor with me and wrapped his arm around me. Within minutes, he fell asleep. It was late, around eleven at night, so the room was dark. I just stared at the ceiling and kept focused on my breathing. 'In, hold and release,' is all I kept telling myself. Suddenly, everything went deep black. No light anywhere. Then, I saw my mom off in the distance. She was wearing that little red bandana dress she made a few months before she died."

"Oh! I remember that!"

"Yep. I'll never forget it. Anyway, a bright intensive white light surrounded her. Yeah, I know how stupid that sounds, but there it was. Anyway, she stood far-off, but I saw her and ran toward her in the light. I know I ran, but I couldn't feel my feet hit the ground. I approached her with my arms extended out and she held her arms out ready to embrace me, you know like in one of those *Hallmark Card* commercials."

Lori snickered. "Yeah. What happened then?"

"Then suddenly, from way back behind me in the darkness, I heard Andrew calling to me. I stopped and looked back to see if it was him. It was, and he kept calling for me to come back. I turned and looked toward Mom. We still hadn't touched, but I could easily touch her hand at this point. I looked deeply into her eyes and I saw and felt pure love there. I missed her so much. I wanted to be with her, but yet, I didn't want to leave Andrew. I looked at her with pleading in my eyes and asked, 'Mom, can Andrew come too?'

"She smiled and tilted her head a little then replied, 'No, sweetie. He can't. You can come with me, or you can go back. The choice is yours.'

"I turned and looked at Andrew, then back at my mother, and asked, 'Mom, would you be mad at me if I went back to him?'

"She shook her head. 'No, the choice is yours.'

"I wanted to hug her so bad, but yet I knew for some reason I shouldn't. So instead, I said, 'I love you, Mom. I'm going to go back to Andrew.'

"My mother nodded her head again, said she loved me and the next thing I knew I was back on the floor lying next to Andrew, who still slept soundly beside me. My asthma had completely vanished. I was one hundred percent fine. As weird as it sounds, that's what I experienced, Lor."

"Wow. So you get a choice?" Lori asked.

"I did that time."

Recalling my experience had left me emotionally exhausted. Our conversation continued for a while, but I was soon out of energy and had to hang up.

"I love you, Bonny."

"I love you too, Lor. Please take it easy and get well. You really don't sound good."

"Okay, mother hen. Don't worry about me, I'm fine. I'm more worried about you."

"Don't be. I already feel better after talking with you. Love you. I'm glad you called. Bye . . . and Merry Christmas. I'll get my letter out to you soon."

"I love your letters, I'll be watching for it."

I rolled over in bed, tired but content. It had been so good to talk with Lori. I had desperately needed that conversation. As she usually did, Lori had lifted me out of my funk. She was the best friend anyone could hope for. But she didn't sound good, and why all the talk about death and crossing over?

29
FINAL CHAPTER

Although I had doctor's approval to work, I still hadn't found a permanent job. Desperate for money to pay off all the medical expenses I'd incurred over the past year, I accepted a ninety-day temporary assignment. When I arrived, I discovered one woman I'd be working with had called in sick—she had the flu. I heard other people cough, sneeze and hack throughout the office. A man walked into my office and immediately coughed then sneezed. Great.

The doctors had told me my immune system was compromised from the medication I currently took as a result of my last hospital visit. They warned me to avoid anyone sick, otherwise, I could land right back in the hospital.

Yet, today was the first day of this temporary job. I desperately needed the money . . . which wasn't much—fifty dollars per day, and after deducting the daily fifteen dollars for gas to travel back and forth, well, my efforts netted me a whopping four dollars and thirty-seven cents an hour—half of the current minimum wage. But, I was desperate. I had all those medical bills to be paid and if I stayed home and worried about them, I knew that would make my asthma worse. I had to keep busy; do something to make me feel that I was working on a solution, or I would go crazy.

I decided I didn't want to start off my temporary position on the wrong foot and jeopardize the job, so I stayed at the office.

I should have listened to the doctors because I caught the flu. I felt it first in my throat, then my ears. I thought, *as long as I don't get the asthma, I can handle this.*

Unfortunately, the asthma joined in the next day. That night I collapsed on the bathroom floor and fought for each breath. My ribs, head and throat hurt. I began to creep in and out of consciousness. Every time I began to slip into the blackness, one of my cats licked my face and brought me back out. I couldn't breathe and I didn't have energy to talk. Terror set in.

I knew I had to get to the hospital or I wouldn't make it through the night. I would die on the bathroom floor and nobody, but my kitties, would know—for possibly days.

I dragged myself to the car and drove the thirty miles to the hospital. By the time I got there, I didn't have the energy to even open the car door. I sat there and begged God to help me breathe.

A security guard came along awhile later and realized I needed help. He got a wheelchair and wheeled me into the ER. I spent the next week in the hospital with the flu complicated by asthma. Good grief. More medical bills I couldn't pay.

Upon release, the doctor gave me strict orders to stay home and away from anyone who coughed, sneezed or even looked ill. I stayed home. That job had just cost me more in medical bills that I would earn over the ninety-day contract.

I was feeling pretty good two weeks later when the house phone rang. I no longer answered that line because it was usually creditors, so it went to the machine. The caller hung up. Then my cell phone rang. Although I didn't recognize the number, I answered.

"Bonny?"

"Yeah. Who's this?"

"Val, Lori's oldest sister."

"Oh wow. Hi Val! How are you?"

"Well . . ." Val hesitated, "I'm calling about Lori."

Suddenly a dread coursed through my body. I began rambling to delay hearing what Val had called about. "Oh no. Did she get in an accident? Or is she sick? The last time I talked with her she sounded terrible. I told her if she didn't take care—"

"*BONNY!*"

"Yeah? What's wrong with Lori?" I asked, praying the dread filling my body was wrong.

"She's dead."

I collapsed into the old green velvet armchair next to my bed. "How?"

"She caught the flu from her husband three days ago." Val's voice changed as she continued. It was as if she was suddenly giving the six o'clock news report. "Yesterday, she got up and fixed Steve's breakfast before he went to work. When he left, Lori was eating cereal and told him she was fine. Marie tried calling her later, but didn't get an answer. She knew Lori had the flu, but also knew it wasn't like her not to answer the phone, so Marie came around to check on her mother. She pounded at the side door, the front door, and walked around the house screaming and hollering. She got no response."

Val stopped and took a deep breath before continuing. "Marie didn't have a key, so called her grandmother—my mom—who told her to try the side door, since the lock didn't always catch. Marie told her she'd already tried it, but Mother insisted she try again. So she went back to the door, pushed on it, and the door swung open."

"Angels at work," I said.

"Anyway, Marie walked in yelling for Lori and found her sitting semi-straight on the edge of the bed holding a washcloth in her hand. Lori was dead."

Once again, that now familiar feeling of numbness began to creep through my body as I visualized Lori on her bed.

"Marie then called EMS and single-handedly got Lori to the floor and began CPR. It was no use. Lori was already dead, and had been so for several hours."

Val's voice faded as my mind wandered back to my last conversation with Lori and all the talk about death and crossing over. When I emerged back to the present, all I could utter was, "This isn't real."

I heard a sob escape from Val. She had tried so hard to keep her emotions in check, but I could sense her strength was weakening. "I wish it weren't. She's my baby sister."

"Oh my God. I'm numb. I can't believe it. This can't be real. I'm the sick one, not Lori. I should be dead, not her! Why her?"

Val inhaled deeply before answering, "I don't have the answer."

Val told me the funeral was being held in Saginaw, but plans were still being made and the family really would appreciate it if I could be there.

I thought about it for a minute. I knew in my heart if I didn't go, I'd regret it forever. Lately, I'd felt okay, yet if I stayed home thinking about missing Lori's service, my thoughts and guilt would probably bring on another attack. I knew what I had to do.

"Of course I'll be there. Marie and Ken need me. I need them. I will be there. That's what the hell credit cards are for—to use when you're broke. I'll be there, Val. Let me pack, and find a cat sitter, and I'll call you when I leave in the morning, okay?"

"Thank you, Bonny," Val said. "Your coming here means the world to all of us. Lori loved you."

"And I love—loved her."

I sat frozen for a few minutes before I dialed Andrew's number.

"Hey, Andrew."

"Bon!"

"Yeah . . . I've got a favor to ask and some news."

"Shoot," Andrew said cheerfully. He had no idea what was about to be dumped in his lap.

"Ah . . . I'm coming to Michigan; should be there in two days. Can I crash at your place?"

"Always, anytime, sweetheart. You know that." I heard Andrew take a drag from a cigarette. "So what brings you back home to Saginaw?"

"Well, that's the news. I don't know how to put it except straight out there."

"Wouldn't have it any other way."

"Andrew, Lori's dead."

"Lori? You mean *our* Lori?"

"Yeah, Lori."

"What the hell happened?" I repeated everything Val had told me, leaving Andrew as shocked as I was.

"Anyway, I'm leaving in the morning and I'll see you in about forty-eight hours."

"It'll be good to see you, Bon . . . but I never, in a million years, thought it would be for this. I love you, hon. Drive safe."

After promising Andrew I would, I walked upstairs like a zombie, got dressed, walked down the forty steps to my car, drove up the road to the little market, purchased some beer and cigarettes—not really even consciously knowing what I was doing.

I came home, sat on the deck, watched the sunlight dance on the lake and then my eyes followed two hawks soar out over the hill country as they floated on the wind. The thought crossed my mind, *it doesn't look like a day for a funeral; it's too pretty out.*

I cracked open a beer and looked up. "Lor, I love you. You're free, sweetie." I raised the beer can toward the sun in a salute and then continued, "No more pain. No more loss. No more sorrow. You have crossed the veil, and I *know* little Maggie Mae is in your arms."

Tears slid down my cheeks, then sobs from deep in my gut escaped. I cried for several minutes, then reached over and lit a cigarette—something I hadn't done in a long, long time—and I enjoyed the hell out of it.

Early the next morning, I called Val. "I'm on the road and heading home."

30
BACK HOME

After two very long days on the highway, I had learned how to drive in winter conditions all over again. Around nine o'clock the evening before the funeral, I pulled into the driveway of Marjorie's home, Lori's middle sister. I was tired. On the trip north my thoughts kept me occupied. Thoughts of Lori, spanning from our early teen years through our last phone call, had replayed in my mind, yet I hadn't cried at all on the trip north. I'd also decided if I didn't get a job soon, as much as I didn't want to, I'd have to file bankruptcy. The devastating debt I had from medical bills, left me no other choice. But, my main concern now was how Marie and Ken and Steve were taking the sudden loss of Lori. I came home, this final time, for them.

Some people, bundled up in coats, stood near the garage smoking cigarettes. I opened up my car door and a blast of frigid January wind greeted me. *Aah, the Michigan I hated.*

"Hey, who's there?" I asked.

"Aunt Bonny! You made it!" A very tall and very grown up Ken came sliding across the ice-covered snow to me. He bent over and wrapped his arms around me and I did the same—giving him that giant bear hug for college graduation, I had so long ago promised Lori.

We both stood there, clinging to one another and crying. This was hard. So hard.

When we slowly released one another, my teeth began chattering. Ken told me to go into the house; everyone would be glad to see me.

All her family was there: Steve, her beloved husband; Marie and Ken, both fine young adults; and her mom, who looked great. Lori's sisters and their husbands, and her brother and his wife were also inside—I hadn't seen them since Lisa's wedding. Also inside were Lori's stepchildren and grandchildren who, until now, I'd only seen in photographs.

The grandchildren chased each other around the house and played games. They were too young to understand what had happened, and sadly, they probably wouldn't remember their grandmother or how much she loved them.

The adults kept busy as they searched through photographs of Lori to use in a PowerPoint presentation and put on a poster board display for the service the next day.

Before I left Texas, I had had enough wits about me to grab my photo albums. I went out into the freezing night air to get them out of the car. Once the family had selected the photos to use, they wrote their speeches for the funeral. They asked me to say something as well. I knew I would say something, but I didn't have a clue what it would be. I'd wing it—the words would be straight from my heart.

Shortly before I left to go to my high school sweetheart's home, Marjorie said something about reading Psalm 23: *Though I walk through the valley of the shadow of death.*

I looked up and said, "That was read at my mom's funeral."

"I suppose it's pretty standard for these things," Val said. "Right after that is read is when you could get up and say a few words."

"Not after that. I'll be in the back of the room crying."

"You will *not* be in the back of the room," Val said. "You are sitting with us. You are family. Don't even think otherwise."

I was so touched. Such a wonderful family! I guess I'd been in Texas longer than I realized because "bless your heart" is all I could think of to say.

I left shortly afterward to go to Andrew's house. It was nearly midnight by the time I knocked on his back door, before letting myself in. He now lived in the yellow house across the street from the high school. It looked exactly the same as it did when Andrew and I would sneak over for lunch nearly forty years ago. However, all around the house the fields had given way to soccer fields, a park and a new housing development. Nothing ever remained the same.

When I stepped into the warmth of Andrew's home, his dogs came to greet me. I petted them and then glanced up— there stood Andrew. We simply looked at each other and then hugged for several minutes. No words were necessary.

That evening Andrew and I had a few beers and a few more cigarettes as we sat in his family room in front of a roaring fire. It was good to see him again. We hadn't seen each other since the high school reunion nearly seven years before.

We talked about the good times with Lori, about how she had changed her life around, how she was so good and loving toward others, how she always saw the good in others and how she had a heart of pure gold. Now, she held Maggie Mae in her arms as she soared with the angels.

Yet, we were both still in disbelief. We toasted to Lori, to friendship, to best friends.

We talked about our lives. Andrew had given up all hope of marriage. He hadn't dated in years. But, then again, neither had I. "The one thing I do regret," he said "is never having a child. I really would have loved to be a parent." He stopped and looked at me, "You are truly blessed to have Jennifer, despite everything. Don't you ever forget that!"

"Oh, I know. I can't even imagine life without her. She's my life's greatest accomplishment."

When we called it a night, I went to his mother's bedroom to sleep. He had lost her just before my father died. We had all gone through so much over the years.

I rose with the sun the next morning. I still couldn't believe I'd come to attend my best friend's funeral. Prior to the service, the casket would be open for family to see and say good-bye to Lori. For the public, it would be a closed casket. I planned to meet her son and husband at the funeral home early that afternoon, so we could say our private goodbyes.

Before heading over there, I took several photographs of Andrew and his dogs. Afterward, I took a drive through town, visited my previous boss at the radio station I had worked at so long ago and was touched when he offered me a job—a job I desperately needed and that sounded fun and challenging. If it had been anywhere but Michigan, I would have accepted his offer in a heartbeat. But I could never return to Michigan. The memories were too painful.

Afterward, I drove the short distance to the next town to visit my mother's grave. I knelt at her stone and wiped the snow away. The sun shone brightly down but did nothing to warm the brutally cold air. Dressed in my open-toed black heels, I had forgotten to bring snow boots, my feet froze as I squatted in the snow-covered grass.

"Mom, it's me. I know you're not here. You're comforting Lori. I know, that you know, she's with you and God now. Is Dad with you too, Mom? I can't even go say good-bye to him. His sister has his ashes. You never liked her, now I know why. I miss you, Mom."

I proceeded to tell Mother about her granddaughter, who had visited her grave once—just before her first driving lesson. The memory brought a brief smile to my face and then I said goodbye, not knowing when, or if, I'd ever be back.

I arrived at the funeral home before Steve and Ken. The thoughtful funeral director offered me coffee, which I willingly accepted . . . I was frozen!

Shortly afterward, Ken walked in with his arm wrapped around Steve. Steve had aged ten years overnight. Together we walked into the room where Lori's casket had been set up. I stood back so Ken and Steve could walk up to Lori first.

I looked around the room. The photo boards were there. Roses, carnations and baby-breath floral arrangements, ceramic angels and poems surrounded the glistening-white casket that had delicately painted pink flowers on the outside and white silk lining inside. Music played softly. I thought it was calmingly beautiful and knew Lori would have liked it.

Ken stayed at the casket, touching his mother's hair as Steve walked back to me.

In a hushed tone, I asked him, "Are you doing okay?"

He collapsed into my arms. "I loved her so much." It took all my strength to hold Steve up. I just let him sob and held him.

"She loved you too, you know."

"I don't think she ever understood how much I loved her. I wasn't real good about showing it."

"She knew. She knows, Steve."

Ken joined us. He put his arm around the only father he had ever really known. My turn had come to say goodbye to my lifelong friend.

I slowly approached the coffin with my hands clasped tightly in front of me. As I gazed down at Lori, I first noticed the beautiful pink satin skirt set she had worn at Ken's wedding. I recognized it from the photographs she had sent of the event. Then, I looked upon her hands gracefully folded over her flat tummy. Her wedding band set sparkled under the spotlight. Her hair, thick as always, still held some traces of blonde. I stood and gazed down upon her face. Her light-brown eyes were shut, behind the familiar wire rim glasses. Her closed lips, a faint shade of pale pink. Suddenly, I realized how often Lori had a smile on her face. In my mind, she smiled. What I saw before me didn't really look like her; just a body that housed a beautiful soul for fifty-four years. The soul was gone now and all that remained was an empty shell.

I reached out and touched her hand. Without a doubt in my mind, I knew Lori was in a better place, holding her beloved dog. She was happy. I felt better.

The rest of Lori's immediate family joined us within minutes. One by one they all went to tell Lori goodbye. Eventually the funeral director came in and lowered the lid of the casket. The time had come to let the public in and soon the service would begin.

Andrew walked up to my side and together we went to take our seats. One more time, I would lean on him. I was thankful to still have him in my life. He'd supported me through my mother's death, my daughter's birth, my divorce, my high school reunions, my father's death, and now, the funeral of my dearest friend in the world.

Although Andrew, Lori and I weren't physically together at the yellow house as Lori had seen in her dream, I knew we were all together in spirit. As Andrew reached over to hold my hand, I could feel Lori smiling down on us. Maybe he felt her too.

Andrew and I sat in the second row, along with Lori's brother in-law and spouses of her stepchildren. In front of us sat her stepdaughter, son, husband and daughter.

The PowerPoint of the photographs rolled across the screen. I watched it through two cycles before I began to look around. Friends and family packed the room. Out in the hall, the funeral director quickly assembled three rows of chairs. Not a seat remained empty. All these lives linked to Lori. I don't think Lori ever realized how deeply she was loved by all she touched. I now understood how truly blessed I was to have had such a wonderful friend for the past forty years. Someone who knew me better than anyone else on this planet—and still liked me! The thought brought a serene smile to my face.

The service began. The funeral director got up and invited the family to say some words, and afterward encouraged others to share their stories about Lori. As the funeral director stepped back, Ken walked up to the podium. Looking down, he unfolded a sheet of paper, took a deep breath, then raised his head to face the mourners and began the eulogy to his mother. I was so proud of him. Such a good, strong, intelligent man he had become. Lori's legacy would live through him.

Lori's sisters, her brother, her stepchildren and her niece spoke in turn. And then others were asked to come forward. I knew I needed to say something. I didn't have any idea what. But I had to.

A woman came forward and stepped behind the podium. She introduced herself as Sue. Taking a deep breath to control her loud sobs, she began, "I'm Steve's first wife, and the mother of Steve's children. I just couldn't let this moment slip by." She stopped to gain composure. "All of you knew Lori, some of us knew her crazy days and ways, but some of you may not know what a truly wonderful person she was. Lori raised my children as her own. Never once did they feel like stepchildren. Never. Lori gave her love unconditionally. She had a heart of gold, and I just wanted all of you to know that." Sue broke down in heart-wrenching sobs. Clutching a tissue to muffle her cries and catch her tears, she slowly stepped away from the podium, with her head hanging down and walked out of the room.

Wow, I knew that about Lori, but for Steve's ex to say it at his current wife's funeral, that was really something. I had to speak. Now.

I stood up and maneuvered around Andrew to approach the podium. I didn't have a clue what I would say, and quite honestly, I don't remember all of what I said. But, some of the words that poured out of me are still in my head: "Lori's heart was as big as Texas and pure gold. She loved her kids and her grandkids—they meant the world to her . . . and I was lucky to have been loved by Lori as well. Our lives were linked for forty years and for that, I am blessed. I now have another angel watching over me."

As I finished, a single tear rolled slowly down my cheek. With the back of my hand, I wiped it off. *I love you, Lor. I'll see ya soon.*

The End

CRCR&D&D

ABOUT THE AUTHOR

For now, Bonny Brookes calls the Texas hill country home.

Inspired by the gorgeous vista of hills, water and daily sunsets, she writes inspirational stories hoping to help others overcome adversity and insurmountable odds.

When not writing or doing volunteer work with animals, she cuddles with her half dozen rescued felines, travels, plays piano or guitar, reads and photographs nature and wildlife.

www.ingramcontent.com/pod-product-compliance
Lightning Source LLC
Chambersburg PA
CBHW031505270326
41930CB00006B/264